Too often, we focus a ton on dating and little on engagement. But the season of engagement is an opportunity for preparation, joy, and evident holiness. In this short and readable book, Sean and Spencer walk the reader through a scripturally faithful approach to this unique season. All around us, people want nothing more than fleeting romance and a little fun. This book will help you to build something grander and greater: a six-decade marriage, a union that testifies to the world of a greater love and a greater God.

—**Owen Strachan**, Associate Professor of Christian Theology, Midwestern Seminary; Coauthor, *The Grand Design: Male and Female He Made Them*

Spencer Harmon and Sean Perron have blessed us with an outstanding book to help couples make the most of their engagement. I am surprised how many couples forget and fail to use their season of engagement to grow together in godliness. Harmon and Perron want to prevent such an oversight, and thus they wisely guide couples through every imaginable step of the engagement journey, providing biblically informed principles along the way. From the kind of ring to buy to preparations for the wedding night, this book is brimming with truth for one of the most critical times in the life of a couple.

—**Jonathan Holmes**, Pastor of Counseling, Parkside Church, Uniontown, Ohio; Author, *The Company We Keep: In Search of Biblical Friendship*

Getting engaged is a monumental decision for your life. Therefore it is worth your careful thought before you take any action. This is the type of book that will stimulate your thinking with biblical guidance before you proceed to make such a serious commitment. We invest years of training before entering a profession—why not take the time to carefully read this book before you commit to marriage and get engaged? We believe that carefully reading this book will biblically inform your decision.

—**John D. and Janie L. Street**, Authors, *The Biblical Counseling Guide for Women*

Sean Perron and Spencer Harmon have written a very practical book for engaged couples and, perhaps just as important, for parents and pastors providing counsel and direction to engaged couples. In words that are perhaps not often used with premarital materials, here is a lot of horse sense on often neglected topics. I commend it to you.

—**Douglas Wilson**, Pastor, Christ Church, Moscow, Idaho

In a culture that is consistently and continually failing miserably at marriage, we desperately need someone to show us a better way. Sean and Spencer, along with their wives, have stepped up to the plate and willingly put their lives on display. *Letters to a Romantic: On Engagement* is down to earth, practical, helpful, and rooted in God's Word. Thank you both for writing this book. We highly recommend it!

—**Kristen Clark and Bethany Baird**, Founders, GirlDefined Ministries; Coauthors, *Girl Defined: God's Radical Design for Beauty, Femininity, and Identity*

Engagement is an exhilarating step toward the unknown with someone you're still getting to know. Where can a couple get wise counsel for a season that ricochets, almost daily, between sparkling anticipation and disorienting discussion? The answer is two guys and a book—the very one in your hands! Pull up a chair and spend a few hours with Sean and Spencer. You will come away packed with fresh faith, enriched by practical insights, and uniquely prepared for the magnificent journey toward marriage!

—**Dave Harvey**, Executive Director, Sojourn Network; Author, *When Sinners Say "I Do": Discovering the Power of the Gospel for Marriage*

Praise for Both *Letters to a Romantic* Books

Sean and Spencer are two old souls. They have a remarkable amount of wisdom to offer on these topics—wisdom well beyond their years. I wholeheartedly recommend anything these two godly men, exemplary husbands, and exceptional leaders have to say about how they met their wives, honored them from courtship into marriage, and now lead and love them in the way of Christ.

—**Dan DeWitt**, Director, Center for Biblical Apologetics and Public Christianity, Cedarville University; Author, *Jesus or Nothing* and *Christ or Chaos*

From romanticism, to breakups, to the issue of sexuality and singleness, Sean and Spencer provide us with a significant, biblical word for the areas of dating and engagement. No two areas are more ignored and yet more in need of a clear, concise word from God. These biblical counselors, with rare insight and discernment, lead you through the spiritual steps that will result in healthy, God-honoring, deepening relationships.

—**Mac and Debbie Brunson**, Cohosts of "The Fixer Upper Marriage" Bible Study, First Baptist Church, Jacksonville, Florida

Relationships require wisdom. God has given Sean and Spencer remarkable wisdom for their age. Their wisdom, seasoned with plenty of Scripture, written in the form of letters from a friend, is a recipe for real help for couples navigating dating and engagement.

—**C. J. Mahaney**, Senior Pastor, Sovereign Grace Church, Louisville, Kentucky

These books contain the kind of wise biblical advice an older brother or mentor would offer to a young person who is seeking to navigate the waters of romance and engagement. Their short-letter format makes them very easy (and fun) to read. Practical answers are given to the questions young people are most likely to raise.

—**Jim Newheiser**, Director of the Christian Counseling Program and Associate Professor of Practical Theology, Reformed Theological Seminary, Charlotte; Executive Director, Institute for Biblical Counseling and Discipleship

Letters to a Romantic: On Dating and *On Engagement* are wonderful guides written by two young men who have a lot of biblical wisdom.

Each letter is engaging and very informative. In fact, they are so good that I have five young adults in mind to give them to. Perron and Harmon have done an exceptional job.

—**Martha Peace**, Biblical Counselor; Author, *The Excellent Wife* and *Damsels in Distress*

There's nothing easy about dating or getting engaged. I lurched through the process like most people—fearful, fumbling, and full of doubt. If only Sean and Spencer had written these books fifty years ago! But here they are just in time for you! Make a date with these books before booking a date. The Bible's advice is never dated for those who are engaged in its teachings.

—**Robert J. Morgan**, Teaching Pastor, The Donelson Fellowship, Nashville; Author, *The Strength You Need: The Twelve Great Strength Passages of the Bible*

In these two books on dating and engagement, Sean Perron and Spencer Harmon have given us a treasure trove of biblically based practical information for all unmarried Christians. I am very grateful to God for giving Sean and Spencer the desire and ability to write these two books. They contain information that I wish had been available for me to give to Christians as they thought about dating or engagement. I will certainly have them at the ready to give to Christians who need biblically based answers to the plethora of relevant issues that godly people who are thinkers will have about these topics.

—**Wayne Mack**, Director and Professor, Strengthening Ministries Training Institute; Director, Association of Certified Biblical Counselors—Africa

Sean Perron and Spencer Harmon are full of wise, gospel-centered counsel on navigating through singleness, dating, and engagement. Whatever your season of life, you will find yourself better equipped to guide others and to strengthen your own faith by reading these books.

—**Russell Moore**, President, Ethics & Religious Liberty Commission of the Southern Baptist Convention

Letters

TO A

Romantic

letters
TO A
Romantic

ON ENGAGEMENT

SEAN PERRON
& SPENCER HARMON

P&R
PUBLISHING
P.O. BOX 817 • PHILLIPSBURG • NEW JERSEY 08865-0817

Scripture quotations are from the *ESV® Bible* (*The Holy Bible, English Standard Version®*), copyright © 2001 by Crossway, a publishing ministry of Good News Publishers. Used by permission. All rights reserved.

Italics within Scripture quotations indicate emphasis added.

Printed in the United States of America

Library of Congress Cataloging-in-Publication Data

Names: Perron, Sean, author.
Title: Letters to a romantic : on engagement / Sean Perron, Spencer Harmon.
Description: Phillipsburg : P&R Publishing, 2017.
Identifiers: LCCN 2017026452| ISBN 9781629953076 (pbk.) | ISBN 9781629953083 (epub) | ISBN 9781629953090 (mobi)
Subjects: LCSH: Marriage--Religious aspects--Christianity. | Betrothal--Religious aspects--Christianity. | Weddings--Planning.
Classification: LCC BV835 .P47 2017 | DDC 248.8/44--dc23
LC record available at https://lccn.loc.gov/2017026452

To the Lambert family:

Jenny and I can't thank you enough for
your investment in us during our engagement.

—Sean

To John Harmon,

who modeled sacrificial love toward
the wife of his youth until the end of his days.

—Spencer

CONTENTS

FOREWORD

You're reading this book because you're thinking about getting married. That is a big and important step. In fact, for most of us, the only decision that is more important than this one is the decision to trust Christ with our salvation. This means that for most people the decision about who to marry is the second most important decision in their entire lives. It concerns the one with whom you promise to spend your life, raise children, share earthly possessions, and experience all the joys and trials of life. It's a big deal.

And you need to be very careful. Let me tell you why.

I have spent a massive amount of time in my ministry doing counseling. Most of that counseling has been with couples who are thinking of getting married or with married couples who are wondering why they got married. Over the years I have noticed a fascinating similarity between pre-marriage counseling and marriage counseling: the topics are the same.

The five most common subjects discussed in marriage counseling are sex, relationships with in-laws, communication and conflict resolution, money, and children and family planning. Pre-marriage counseling is about thinking and preparing for these exact issues before you get married. The most significant difference between the way these topics are covered in pre-marriage counseling and the way they are addressed in remedial marriage counseling is that couples are still in a good mood about these issues before they get married. Typically, engaged couples are excited to think about these issues and plan for them, because they are eager to experience them together. When the same issues come up again years after the wedding and require marriage counseling, there is much more pain in the discussion.

So you need to be very careful to take the time to address these issues before they become problems. But right now you're probably facing a temptation that is very common during this time of preparation.

Most people in your position are tempted to spend this season thinking only about the wedding. You feel pressured to focus on planning the reception, reserving the church, and ordering the clothes and food. You need to fight against this temptation. It is far more important to focus on your marriage. The wedding will be over in a few hours; the marriage will endure for years and years.

This book is written with the intent of helping you to cut through the noise of wedding planning so that you can do the crucial work of marriage preparation. The time you spend right now laying the groundwork for your life with your spouse will reap incredible dividends later. The central aim of this book is to help you, by God's grace, to produce the dividends of a Christ-honoring marriage for years to come.

After fourteen years of marriage, my wife and I still talk with joy about the valuable lessons we learned about Jesus, life, and marriage during the months of our pre-marriage preparation. At that time we were shocked at what we did not know and grateful for all the lessons we were able to learn. I know that *Letters to a*

Romantic: On Engagement will give you similar joy as you take in the wisdom of its authors.

I first met Sean Perron and Spencer Harmon when they were college students in my marriage and family class at Boyce College. They were young men marked by obvious godliness. In the years since, I have only grown in admiration for them as I have watched them pursue, in a righteous way, the godly women who ultimately became their wives. It has been a tremendous joy over the years to watch as these faithful students became faithful husbands, fathers, and ministers of the gospel. I do not know two young men with more wisdom on these matters.

So shut the catalog full of wedding invitations, close the Google search for wedding cakes, and begin investing in your marriage. Grab your Bible and then turn to the next page of this book to receive the kind of wisdom you'll be talking about with your spouse for the rest of your marriage. The time that you invest now will not be wasted.

Heath Lambert
Jacksonville, FL
August 2016

INTRODUCTION

OUR STORIES OF ROMANCE AND THIS BOOK

Sean and Spencer

Dear Reader,

It was the day of my wedding. And I was not marrying the girl of my dreams.

If you had told me when I was a teenager that my wife would have seven tattoos and a history in drugs, alcohol, and heavy metal concerts, I would have laughed at you, given you one of my courtship books, and told you to take a hike. My plans were much different, much more nuanced, much more clean-cut . . . much more, well, about me.

You see, it wasn't my dream to marry a girl who was complicated. I never dreamed that I would sit on a couch for pre-marital counseling with my future wife and listen to her cry, tell stories of drunken nights, list the drugs she had used, and confess mistakes she had made in past relationships.

It wasn't my dream—it was better.

Many people wouldn't put Taylor and me together. In high school, we probably would not have been friends. Taylor probably would have thought I was a nice, boring, judgmental Christian kid; I probably would have thought she was a nice, lost, party-scene girl who guys like me were supposed to stay away from. People like us, with our backgrounds and histories, are not supposed to meet, fall in love, and covenant their lives to each other.

But everything changes when people meet Jesus. Jesus takes people like rebellious teenage partiers and goody-two-shoes homeschoolers and puts them together in marriage in order to display something much bigger than their own handcrafted, perfectly planned love stories.

Right in the middle of the mess of life, Taylor met Jesus, and he planted his flag in her life. She believed in him, and he transformed her. The woman who spent her life living from one pleasure to the next died, and a new person was born—a new person with new desires and a new heart that longed to please God, serve people, and treasure Jesus Christ above pleasure.

And this is how I see Taylor. She is completely new, completely transformed, and completely clean. This is not because she became a part of a helpful program or because she really "pulled herself together." It's because God, in his incredible, infinite kindness, took Taylor's dark, crimson life and made her as white as snow. He took all of her sins, placed them on his Son, and gave her Jesus' righteousness to wear like a perfect white wedding dress.

In reality, Taylor's story is my story as well. As my wife walked down the aisle toward me that day, I was reminded of how much I did not deserve the precious gift that she was to me. I had spent much of my life singing a self-centered siren song. Nothing about my life cried for blessings; it called for curses forever. Yet God dressed me in white, put my sin upon his Son, and gave me a heart that loves him.

I love Taylor with all that I am. She is gentle, kind, patient, joyful, beautiful, and loving. I didn't deserve to marry someone like her. I never planned for this, but I'm so glad that I did not get what I planned for.

I'm not sure whether your plans are similar to or different from my old plan. Maybe you are in my old shoes—seeking to control all the factors of your relationships in order to make sure you get the spouse who fits your plans. Maybe you are in Taylor's shoes—transformed by grace but wondering how your history will play out in dating, engagement, and marriage. Maybe you are somewhere in the middle.

God has a stunning plan for you: he wants to put his grace on display uniquely in your life and relationships so that other people will praise him (see Eph. 1:5–6). He wants to put his grace on display in every facet of your life—including your engagement.

Until then,
Spencer

Dear Reader,

It took over a year and a half for Jenny to allow me to date her. You would not believe how many times I asked her if we could be in a relationship. My count is thirteen, while hers is at least seventeen attempts. I would have been a complete and total creeper, except that when I asked her to date she said, "No . . . not yet." Her character and beauty mesmerized me, and I was willing to hang on tight to any ounce of hope that we could be together.

We first met in high school and eventually began dating in college. We were engaged for eight months and married at the end of my junior year. We were both twenty-one years old. Our wedding day was the happiest day of our lives, and we simply would not trade marriage for anything.

I would love to tell you that I did everything right when pursuing Jenny for marriage. I would love to tell you that I never blew it and that I always knew what to do in our relationship. I would also love to tell you that I did everything right in my romantic relationships *before* meeting Jenny. But I cannot say all these things.

Jenny and I had many questions. We needed wisdom. There were moments that were complex, confusing, and unclear. In the midst of many dangers, joys, and snares, we needed help. Our help came through the sufficient Scriptures and the guidance of dear mentors who loved the Bible. The help we received, particularly while we were engaged, came from people who were willing to take the time to examine our lives in light of God's Word.

This is why Spencer and I have decided to write you letters. Although our stories are different, the thread of God's grace runs through both. We have experienced the power of God's Word in engagement and believe that the Bible has real things to say to you during this season of your life.

The book begins right before the proposal takes place, and it takes you all the way to the wedding night. There is an intentional order to the chapters, but the letters can also be read individually according to your needs. Each chapter is designed to be short and practical but not comprehensive. Even though we don't know the specifics of your situation, we have made a concerted effort to make the chapters as relevant as possible. It is our prayer that this content will be immediately helpful and tangible rather than overly narrow or rigid. Our wives, Jenny Perron and Taylor

Harmon, have also contributed to many of the letters and have provided their own warm touches throughout.

Our prayer is that your plans for engagement would begin to align with God's plans to glorify his Son in the world. We pray that these letters will tune your ears to hear God's voice in his Word and will provoke many conversations between you, your partner, and godly mentors in your lives.

We are not relational gurus. Quite the opposite. We would be the first to admit to you that when we follow our own wisdom we get lost. We are sinners who are desperately in need of God's illuminating Word in every facet of our lives. We have simply tasted the goodness of God's shepherding voice in our romances, and we want you to taste it too. We pray that you fall in love with hearing his voice in the Bible so that it guides you in engagement—and in every other season to come.

Until then,
Sean

THE OPPORTUNITY
OF ENGAGEMENT

Sean

Dear Romantic,

You've agonized over whether to date. You've dated. There have been moments of fun and deep joy, and there have been moments of difficulty and hard conversations.[1] You have sought to follow Christ as you've pursued romance, and now the time has come. You sense that marriage is on the horizon.

Your wedding day is arguably the most important day of your life. As you prepare to propose to your potential bride or to respond to a proposal from your potential husband, don't miss the greatest opportunity that engagement has to offer. Engagement is an excellent time to pause and consider what is about to take place.

---

1. If you are still considering whether or not you should marry the person you are dating, we recommend reading the first book in this series, *Letters to a Romantic: On Dating* (Phillipsburg, NJ: P&R, 2017).

When a couple unites in marriage, they fully give themselves to each other. The wife gives everything that she has to her husband, and the husband gives everything that he has to his wife. Our union with Christ is similar. Through his death, burial, and resurrection, everything that we have (sin, shame, guilt, and death) becomes Christ's and everything that he has (purity, holiness, freedom, and life) becomes ours.

The following quote has stuck with me for several years. It is an old quote from Martin Luther.[2] On the topic of marriage, he writes, "Now if they are one flesh, and if a true marriage . . . then it follows that all they have becomes theirs in common, as well good things as evil things; so that whatsoever Christ possesses, that the believing soul may take to itself and boast of as its own, and whatever belongs to the soul, that Christ claims as His."[3] This is the sweet exchange that Luther is talking about: "If I have sinned, my Christ, in whom I believe, has not sinned; all mine is His, and all His is mine; as it is written: 'My beloved is mine, and I am His.'"[4]

All of our sins become Christ's, and all of His righteousness becomes ours. Many people think of the gospel as only providing forgiveness, but the gospel also gives us the righteous state of Jesus (see 2 Cor. 5:21). His perfect life becomes our life, while our sinful life became His on the cross. This forgiveness and righteousness is obtained only by "the wedding ring of faith."

Your marriage will not be based on the condition of works. No one will submit a list of good deeds at the altar. You will not swap resumes; you will exchange rings. You will become husband

2. See Martin Luther, *Christian Liberty* (1520; repr., Philadelphia: Lutheran Publication Society, 1903) 13–19, available online at http://books.google.com (search for "Christian Liberty").

3. Ibid, 17.

4. Ibid, 19.

and wife by a simple pledge of faith. "Thus the believing soul, by the pledge of its faith in Christ, becomes free from all sin, fearless of death, safe from hell, and endowed with the eternal righteousness, life, and salvation of its husband Christ."[5] As you prepare to take each other's hands in faith, take the hand of Christ by faith. Pledge your life to Him, trusting not in your good works or good intentions but only in His perfect life and saving death.

Christ did not buy you with precious metal but with His priceless blood. Engagement is a wonderful opportunity to ponder the greater privilege of being united to Christ. So before we begin with the details, let's stand in awe with Luther: "Who then can value highly enough these royal nuptials? Who can comprehend the riches of the glory of this grace?"[6]

Until then,
Sean

DISCUSSION QUESTIONS

1. Have you paused in the midst of your busy schedule and thanked God for how he created marriage?
2. Are you currently trusting in Christ *alone* for salvation from sin, death, and God's wrath?
3. List two ways that your upcoming marriage points toward the good news of Jesus.

5. Ibid, 18.
6. Ibid., 18–19.

THE COST OF ENGAGEMENT

Sean

Dear Brother,

You are about to propose. You have settled the question of *who* you want to marry, and now you are working on the details of *how* you are going to get her to say yes. These are exciting days.

In Western culture, it is customary for you to drop to one knee and present a ring to your hopeful bride-to-be when you ask for her hand in marriage. In one sense, this is a small detail in the engagement process. It is just a round piece of metal that slips around a finger. In another sense, however, this is a massive component.

The ring signifies a change in relationship status. Your future bride will be wearing *your* engagement ring and no one else's. It is from you to her. In the not-so-distant future, *you* will place a wedding band on her finger. Not only that, but everyone and their mothers will look at this small piece of jewelry. They will ooh and ahh, giggle and gasp at the sight of your fiancée's ring. Photos of this ring will be liked, and statuses will be shared. It is a statement to everyone who sees your fiancée that she is about to become *yours*.

But now the practical questions begin to arise. What kind of ring should you buy? How much money should you spend? Are there priorities when it comes to ring shopping?

These types of questions are not limited to wedding rings. You will be faced with such financial questions before, during, and after this season of engagement. There are three basic categories that may help you in the days ahead as you are faced with questions about spending money. First, make sure that you and your partner know each other well. Second, seek to store up more treasure in heaven than on earth. Third, don't be ashamed to receive good gifts from God and others.

KNOW YOUR FIANCÉE

When it comes to buying a ring, it is not about you. It is about her. What will your fiancée want? What will make her feel most loved? Not all fiancées are created equal when it comes to monetary possessions. Therefore, it is your job to know *your* fiancée.

Let's take the example of the engagement ring. There are godly women who want a beautiful diamond ring to wear around their finger and display to the world. This isn't necessarily because they are flashy or ritzy. They see great value in having a lifelong token of marital love that represents beauty and value. If your fiancée is like this, she will be sorely disappointed if you can afford a nice ring but decide to go cheap. You want your ring to communicate "I love you and I know you," not "I did the bare minimum to get by."

On the other hand, your fiancée might actually prefer something more frugal. I know women who prefer a pearl wedding ring instead of a diamond ring. They would rather the ring be a symbol of love that isn't defined by earthly riches. They would genuinely prefer to save $1,000 and spend it on something else.

If your fiancée feels this way, an expensive ring might actually distract her from the true value that the ring holds. She would want something unique and special and wouldn't necessarily feel loved just because you dropped a lot of cash.

Of course, you don't want to propose to a girl who is going to base her decision on the kind of ring you offer her. If she starts to ask about the karats of the gold when you ask for her hand in marriage, then you'd better get off your knee and tell her that you need more time as well. An engagement isn't based on a ring, but a ring should be a thoughtful, well-planned, and cherished token of love.

I think I paid $250 for Jenny's engagement ring. (And this was in 2011, not 1911.) I bought a gold ring with three small diamonds that someone was selling on our college bulletin board. Everyone who thought I was crazy didn't really know Jenny—she loves simple. Jenny loves that ring. You can ask her yourself. I could have spent $2,500 on a nicer ring, and she would have asked why we hadn't saved that money for something else. I knew that finding a simple, beautiful, and inexpensive ring would best communicate my affection to my future wife. But you aren't marrying Jenny. She is taken. You need to find out what your fiancée loves and wants deep down.

These questions aren't pertinent to only wedding rings. You will soon find yourself faced with a myriad of items that need to be purchased for your big day. There will be cakes to taste, venues to consider, and clothes to pick out. All of these things will require money and will make some sort of statement to onlookers.

STORING AND RECEIVING TREASURE

When it comes to these kinds of things, I encourage you to store up your treasure in heaven, where moth and rust will not destroy and where thieves will not break in and steal (see Matt. 6:19–21). Your wedding day is *one day*, and that day lasts only twenty-four hours. You don't have to spend a year's salary on your wedding in order to make it special. You don't need silver and gold to reflect God. Jesus loves to shine in things like clay pots and broken vessels (see 2 Cor. 4:7).

But don't be ashamed to receive good gifts (see James 1:17). If your parents want to pour out their love on you with expensive dishes and beautiful flower arrangements, don't be an overspiritual snob. Jesus wasn't. Jesus knew how to receive good gifts. He let the woman anoint his feet with expensive perfume that was worth a year's salary. He created excellent wine at a wedding he attended (see John 2:1–11). It is a good and holy thing to thankfully receive gifts from those who want to give them.

You will be faced with a lot of purchases in the days ahead. Buying a ring is just the beginning. With every investment of your money, be sure to know your partner well, store up more treasure in heaven than on earth, and not be ashamed to receive good gifts from God and others.

Until then,
Sean

DISCUSSION QUESTIONS

1. Will your fiancée feel loved by a simple ring or by a more expensive ring? Why?
2. What do wedding purchases reveal about your hearts? Where do you and your fiancée store up treasure?
3. Do you have a hard time receiving expensive gifts from others? Why or why not?

THE DETAILS OF ENGAGEMENT

Spencer

Dear Romantic,

Apartments, cars, bank accounts, jobs, churches, families, children, debt, your remaining education, money. These are just a few of the concerns that arise during marriage. During the season of engagement, your joy about marriage also comes with responsibility. You are joining your lives together, and the process of the two becoming one can be stressful and expensive.

During engagement, it can be difficult to see how everything is going to come together in time for you to get married. There is a countdown to the big day, and you may still need to find an apartment. You might be nervous because both of you are bringing some debt into the marriage. You are both financially responsible people who work hard to afford life together. Yet a pit still forms in your stomach when you think about all the possible expenses and unknowns that could arise in marriage.

HUMILITY IN THE HUSTLE

Engagement brings vulnerability. You can certainly sense it. There is the vulnerability of love—your heart is so intertwined with your fiancé's that the thought of something happening to this person takes your breath away. Yet there is also the vulnerability brought on by need. In engagement, we can often sense our needs in a greater way than we did when we lived our single lives. We see the resources needed, the communication expected, and the intimacy anticipated, and we wonder how we can provide it all.

Seasons like engagement are meant to bring you to the end of yourself. We always need God's provision, but sometimes he is gracious enough to let us tangibly feel it. He designs to bring us to the end of ourselves so that we might hope in him (see 2 Cor. 1:8–11). God often uses trying seasons like engagement in order to humble us. He desires to show us what has always been true: that we are desperately dependent on him for all of life.

Instead of speculating about what would happen if all the resources did not come in on time, calm and quiet your soul. Don't occupy yourself with things too great for you (see Ps. 131), but trust in the Lord. In this season, answer your "what ifs" with "God will." What if we don't have enough money at the beginning of our marriage? God will provide for all your needs according to his riches and glory in Christ Jesus (see Phil. 4:19). What if we don't have enough time together because of busy schedules? God will give you wisdom when you ask for it in faith (see James 1:5). God's promises are greater than your speculations. God knows, and God cares. He feeds the birds, clothes the flowers, and meets the needs of his children (see Matt. 6:25–33).

God is calling you to trust him with your most significant

needs. However, that does not mean that you sit back, fold your hands, and look at the clouds. The comforting words of God's provision are always accompanied by the prodding words of the Proverbs. "Go to the ant," says Solomon to his son. "Without having any chief, officer, or ruler, she prepares her bread in summer and gathers her food in harvest" (Prov. 6:6–8). In seasons of great need, God calls us not only to trust him but also to get moving.

GET TO WORK

The ant is so imitable because it prepares beforehand for the task ahead. Although the future is daunting and you are not sure where all the resources will come from, keep your head down and continue working. Don't let your anxiety keep you from productivity. Use the season of engagement to prepare for marriage with all your might.

Are you concerned about finances? Sit down on a date night and use an Excel spreadsheet to crunch numbers together. Are there any expenses you can cut? Are there any side jobs you can get? Make a budget that can accommodate two people and realize that you both may need to make sacrifices in order to live life together as a newly married couple.

Are you worried about time? Get your calendars out and project what your lives will look like after marriage. What shifts do each of you work? Where are the free times in your schedules? Are there commitments that you need to cut in order to spend regular time together? Use your calendar, cut the loose ends, and redeem the time. Are you worried about getting all the details of your wedding done? Write all the tasks down, and then unashamedly employ the help of church friends and family members. Remove the fog with concrete actions.

As you look at your finances and time commitments, show your pre-marriage counselor what you find. Let older, wiser saints bear your burdens with you. Wisdom cries out in the streets (see Prov. 1:20). Are you listening?

THE SPARROWS SING

Jesus is unsurpassed in providing for his children's needs, but his definition of *needs* is different from ours. God wants you to trust him in this season and to cast all your burdens on him. When the cares of your heart are many, God promises to comfort you (see Ps. 94:19). Do not neglect to sit at the feet of Jesus and calm your busy heart with the promises of his provision. The sparrows sing because they do not worry about tomorrow— God will provide for them. Let the consolations of the Lord's provision fill you with a new song to sing as you see him act on your behalf. Let your heart swell with faith as your Father meets all your needs.

Until then,
Spencer

DISCUSSION QUESTIONS

1. What is more difficult for you: trusting God in humility or getting to work? Why?
2. What decisions still need to be made about your future?
3. Have you asked older people in your life to view your monthly budget?

THE LENGTH OF ENGAGEMENT

Spencer

Dear Romantic,

It's an amazing thing, isn't it? Soon your partner is going to be your spouse. You've prayed, dreamed, and hoped, and now you get to set a date when you will finally be one with the person you love.

You are probably already noticing that there are a lot of factors that surface during wedding planning. Creating a gift registry, finding a venue, asking your pastor to officiate, and selecting your bridal party—all the while honoring the opinions of family and friends who want to be a part of the big day. The sheer amount of things that must be done to prepare for the big day has forced you to consider whether or not you should extend your engagement. Should you have a longer engagement?

Let me say up front that the length of your engagement is not an issue of sin and righteousness. I have friends who were engaged for four months and others who were engaged for close to two years. There are a myriad of unique situations that could necessitate a long engagement for you and your spouse. My hope is to provide some categories for you to consider as you make this decision together.

LONG ENGAGEMENTS INTENSIFY DESIRE

What makes the wedding day so exciting? It's all about the waiting. Everyone who attends knows that the bride and groom have waited for this day. Anticipation builds as the audience watches the groom wait at the altar for the doors to open and the bride to walk into the room. Waiting has a way of building excitement that makes the wedding day electric.

Waiting also has a flip side that you are already experiencing: longing. Longing is what gives waiting its intensity. The reason that magazines and TVs are placed in waiting rooms is to distract us from having to wait for our appointments. But even these distractions can occupy us for only so long before we twiddle our thumbs, grow restless, and demand to be called.

Engagement is charged with longing. You probably noticed that after you proposed to your fiancé the yearning for marriage suddenly rushed on you. The engagement period only reinforces these longings. You begin to plan your life together during a season of separation. It feels wrong to say goodbye at the end of every night, because you are preparing for relational nearness. It is frustrating (and expensive!) to constantly drive each other to "safe zones" so you can plan the wedding together but not be alone. On top of all this, you have a good and growing physical desire for your fiancé, and you long to experience intimacy in the covenant of marriage. These are strong longings that are supposed to be there and are meant to drive you into marriage.

Long engagements intensify these longings in an unnecessary and unhelpful way. Although the Bible is clear that we are to control our bodies (see 1 Thess. 4:4), I believe that Scripture urges us to satisfy our longings in the right context. In 1 Corinthians 7:9, Paul commands the unmarried to marry if they are not able to exercise self-control. He urges Christians to satisfy their strong longings in a God-honoring way, not to stifle their longings and "burn with passion." The point is that burning with passion leads to temptation and sin. Better to marry than to burn.

CLEARING THE PATH

There are several real and practical concerns that can become obstacles on the path toward marriage. These are significant concerns, but you should not feel required to extend your engagement because of them.

Wedding Planning. Recent conversations with your family have burdened you with the weight of everything that must be done for the wedding. Both of your families have "nonnegotiables" that they believe must be part of a wedding. "There just isn't enough time!" you think. However, you must remember that this is not their wedding or even *your* wedding. This wedding is about God. People may plague you about the details of your wedding, but you are responsible to consider those core elements that will glorify the Lord and serve those who attend. If you strip away all the nonessential details, how much time will it take?

School Commitments. It's often stressful for couples to consider planning for a wedding to take place while one of the partners is still in school. Wouldn't it be easier if you just waited until graduation? It probably would be. However, this is a key time for you to prioritize your longings. Within your family there will always be competing commitments and desires, and you will consistently need to choose which ones you will pursue. I suggest considering an alternative plan for finishing school. Some couples extend their school plan from one year to two in order to focus on building a good marital foundation.

Family Pressure. Your desire to get married sooner rather than later can catch family members off guard. Maybe you have heard some passing remarks about the possibility of extending the engagement. Perhaps people are wondering why you are in such a "hurry." Perhaps they are even right to wonder! Setting the date of your wedding, however, is a decision that ultimately needs to be made by you and your partner. To be sure, you should receive the counsel of your parents, but making this decision together may be a time for you to begin functioning as your own family.

WHAT'S MOST IMPORTANT?

Your wedding planning can function as a practice round for some key aspects of your marriage. Whether it concerns how you manage money, parent your children, or set a date for your wedding, deciding what is most important will always be a discussion in your home.

Consider your longings and prioritize them biblically. The Lord promises to give wisdom to everyone who asks, and as you make this decision together he will provide you everything you need.

Until then,
Spencer

DISCUSSION QUESTIONS

1. What are the pressures that push you toward a longer engagement?
2. What are your current priorities in wedding planning?
3. Are there things you are prioritizing that could be cut out of your plans?

BAD ADVICE

Sean

Dear Romantic,

One thing I noticed while I was engaged was that everyone has a story. Every couple has an experience to tell or a word to give. It felt like every person who ever *thought* about being married had something to offer to help me prepare for the rough days ahead.

Most of the advice we received was good, but some of it was not. At one point, Jenny and I felt like we were drowning in "advice." Friends, family, and even strangers had taken it upon themselves to tell us everything someone else had told *them*. Honeymoon horror stories, scary identity-crisis catastrophes, and terrible toothpaste and toilet-seat fiascos.

One person told us to beware the second week of marriage: "The first week is great, but just you wait . . . week number two gets awful." Another person said that the second week was fine but that we had better watch out for that second month. We figured we should start ignoring some of these people when another couple warned us of the dreaded six-month mark.

Evidently, that's when the wildebeests come out and devour all the happy marriages of the world.

I've mentioned only the tip of the iceberg. I would be ashamed to tell you some of the counsel we were given. Nevertheless, I must also tell you that we received some very good advice as an engaged couple. Some of the most precious guidance I received was in pre-marriage counseling. The wonderful encouragement I received from some people almost brings me to tears when I think about it now.

So how can you tell the difference between bad counsel and good counsel? My main suggestion is to know the source. Know the well from which you are seeking water, and don't drink from every running brook.

It is true that "without counsel plans fail, but with many advisers they succeed" (Prov. 15:22). Take note when the Scripture says, "Where there is no guidance, a people falls, but in an abundance of counselors there is safety" (Prov. 11:14).

We should be people who seek the safety of many ropes. However, let us be careful not to be strangled among them. The Proverbs also say, "Good sense is a fountain of life to him who has it, but the instruction of fools is folly" (Prov. 16:22).

To stay safe when dealing with good and bad counselors, you must have sturdy ropes. Holding onto unraveling ropes will only do you harm. It is possible to unwittingly surround yourself with fools.

I suggest that the best place to find counselors is in the local church. Seek out your pastors in particular. "Obey your leaders and submit to them, for they are keeping watch over your souls, as those who will have to give an account" (Heb. 13:17).

The author of wisdom can be found in only one place: the Bible. Listen to those who spend their lives in the Scriptures. Value their opinions, and compare what they say to what you read in the Bible (see Acts 17:11). Starting this habit now will create a great pattern for your future marriage. Prepare now for a lifetime of seeking the Scriptures and rappelling with those who know them well.

May the Scriptures tune our ears to receive good counsel. Whether we receive advice from our parents, pastors, or peers, let us make sure we have ears to hear.

Until then,
Sean

DISCUSSION QUESTIONS

1. On a scale of 1 to 10, how biblically equipped are you to discern foolish advice from wise counsel?
2. What are some indicators that a person is a wise counselor? What are some characteristics of a godly advisor?

GOOD ADVICE

Sean

Dear Romantic,

The single most important action that Jenny and I took before our wedding day was to seek out pre-marriage counseling. That is not an overstatement. Pre-marriage counseling revolutionized our lives and has been the glue that has kept our marriage together. Our counseling walked us through nearly every phase of marriage in advance. We discussed everything from the decision to get married to contraception and children. Our advisors challenged and stretched us for the glory of God.

Jesus used the analogy of a wise king assessing his army before going into battle (see Luke 14:31). He also said that a wise buyer typically sizes up his bank account before making a large purchase (Luke 14:28). Since marriage doesn't come with a return policy, it is best practice to count the cost before moving forward. It would be foolish not to seek out counsel from older, godly couples who have already journeyed down this path.

Now you might be thinking, *It's a busy season, and I can't squeeze another thing into the schedule.* Or you might simply want to get hitched, enjoy the honeymoon, and then consider getting some advice later. Wouldn't it better to wait until after all the passion and pressure has passed? Many marriages over many moons have survived without pre-marriage counseling—why can't yours?

Here are four compelling reasons to begin pre-marriage counseling sooner rather than later.

1. PRE-MARRIAGE COUNSELING SETS THE BANQUET TABLE

Pre-marriage counseling is like setting a beautiful banquet hall. Imagine you and your future spouse receiving an invitation to a royal feast. You arrive to see that the turkey has been seasoned and exquisitely prepared. The candles are glowing, and the tablecloths are spotless and steamed. The chairs are polished, and the silverware sparkles under a diamond chandelier. On top of this, the atmosphere is spectacular. You know that this feast will be truly enjoyable.

Ask yourself this: does a royal feast simply happen? All the glory of such a banquet can be attributed to the preparation that was put into it. If nothing had been prepared, it would have turned out to be an embarrassing disaster: a microwaved dinner on a crusty, plastic TV tray that simply got the job done.

Pre-marriage counseling has the potential to turn your marriage into a banquet hall for feasting instead of a greasy fast-food restaurant. The time you invest in reading books, attending biblical counseling sessions, and working through problems now will bring incredible dividends later on.

The best time for counseling is before a problem arises. Some couples get this counseling before they are engaged, while others get it afterward. Biblical counseling at any stage is beneficial, but the most helpful counsel comes before a crash. It is always better to receive counsel like a seat belt instead of like an ambulance. There is a time for everything—including counseling. And it is always better to be prepared before the problem arises.

2. PRE-MARRIAGE COUNSELING DETERMINES THE GUESTS

Pre-marriage counseling is also helpful in determining whether two particular people should actually enter into the covenant of marriage. Butterflies, birds, and bees all buzz around a wedding ceremony. Emotions are high, and feelings are in full swing. Pre-marriage counseling has the potential to push beyond the present and to bring a long-term vision of marriage into the conversation.

In keeping with the banquet-hall analogy, receiving counseling before marriage enables a couple to determine whether they truly want to RSVP. Many couples enter into engagement without ever thinking through critical questions about conflict resolution or life goals. I have sat with couples in my living room who came for pre-marriage counseling only to realize that they shouldn't get married.

Pre-marriage counseling can help a couple solidify the commitment they made to each other when they got engaged, or it can help them see that they made a decision without thinking through all the ramifications. No one wants a failed engagement, but it is always better to break off an engagement than to file divorce papers.

3. PRE-MARRIAGE COUNSELING DISTINGUISHES THE GUESTS

Picture you and your bride walking out for the first dance without knowing how to dance. This would certainly put a damper on things. It would also be embarrassing if all the proper utensils were arranged but the guests were unfamiliar with basic etiquette.

Pre-marriage counseling helps train couples to love each other biblically and effectively. It pinpoints and seeks to strengthen areas of weakness in each person's life.

There is no shame in requesting help from others. Perhaps you need help in knowing how to be slow to speak and quick to hear. You might need help working through previous sexual sin or being prepared to serve your spouse on your wedding night. There are hundreds of different areas in which you may need instruction. Pre-marriage counseling might be the avenue that God uses to distinguish you and refine your "manners" so that you can thoroughly enjoy the feast.

4. PRE-MARRIAGE COUNSELING HONORS THE HOST

Everything leads to this final purpose—bringing honor to the wedding host. Pre-marriage counseling helps fulfill the Great Commission that Christ laid before the disciples in Matthew 28:18–20. Jesus has commissioned his disciples to teach others everything that he commanded them. *Everything* includes all the intricacies of a Christian marriage. Pre-marriage counseling is a gospel opportunity for you to be taught in the ways of Christ.

It is no secret that God invented marriage for his own glory. Jesus designed every facet of the feast of marriage, from the invitation to the consummation. Every dinner napkin is folded for his fame. Jesus cares about all the details because his honor is at stake.

This also means that pre-marriage counseling is eventually self-perpetuating. Every newly discipled couple is launched out into the world ready to impact others. Through this opportunity, husbands and wives become counselors and in turn teach the next generation of engaged couples. Those who experience the benefits of good, biblical pre-marriage counseling become part of a chain reaction that continues for years to come.

Have you benefited from a godly couple pouring into your life? If not, take this opportunity to seek out rich wisdom before your wedding. The local church is the best place to find this kind of help. Go ahead and reach out to one of your pastors or church leaders, and ask them to do your pre-marriage counseling. It is time to set the table.

Until then,
Sean

DISCUSSION QUESTIONS

1. How can you make time in your schedule for counseling?
2. Who are some trustworthy pastors or mentors who can prepare you for marriage? Is there anyone in your local church whom you respect and trust who could do this?
3. Check out Wayne Mack's excellent workbook for pre-marriage counseling: *Preparing for Marriage God's Way: A Step-by-Step Guide for Marriage Success Before and After the Wedding* (Phillipsburg, NJ: P&R Publishing, 2013). Jenny and I used this workbook and can't recommend it enough.

TILL DEATH DO US PART

Sean

Dear Romantic,

When the time comes for you to stand before your spouse and say your vows, a mix of emotions will flood your soul. The exchange of vows is a weighty thrill. You will be excited by your deep love for your future spouse and yet will feel the sobering weight of your promise.

My heart was full and my mind was racing minutes before I stood on the stage to marry Jenny. I was realizing the permanence of the decision and feeling the heaviness of my inadequacy. I knew the importance of making a lifelong commitment and knew I could never keep my wedding vows without the help of the Holy Spirit.

I want to draw your attention to the line in your vows that says "till death do us part." Not many couples realize the significance of this short phrase.

If you have never contemplated the significance of those five words, then you are not prepared to say them. Marriage does not come with a thirty-day free trial. No one gets a test drive.

The union of marriage is not a mere contract that can be discarded whimsically or viciously. Marriage is a covenant made before God and is not designed to be torn apart. It is made to last a lifetime.

If you say the phrase "till death do us part," you are committing never to leave or forsake your bride until the day you breathe your last. You are pledging to be united until one or both of you see Jesus face to face.

This means that when your partner gets sick and they are unable to care for themselves, you are called "to have and to hold." When your spouse becomes angry and does not communicate with kindness, you are required "to love and to cherish." When life is raw beyond imagination and stressful to the core, you are not allowed to give up on each other.

God designed it this way for our good and his glory. We long for loyal love. We yearn for a love that will not let us go. Consider the following scenarios by asking yourself these questions:

- If you were frail and unable to move your broken body, would you want your spouse to hold you?
- If you were blinded by sin, would you want your spouse to love you until you came to repentance?
- If you were ruined financially and socially, would you want your spouse to remain by your side?

Deep down, every person wants to hear the precious words "I will never leave you nor forsake you." Do you want to hear these words? Do you want to be these words for someone else?

Be warned. The promise is not "till adultery do us part." Nor is it "till abandonment do us part." Regardless of your view of divorce, I plead with you to discard any notion of a "rip cord" in your marriage. Remove from your mind all reasons for divorce and live with each other as Christ does with his bride—without exceptions. Love without an asterisk. Give yourself away without an escape. Be irrevocably committed.

Even when we commit adultery against him, Christ will never leave nor forsake his bride. Even when we abandon our first love, Christ will never abandon his wife. When we play the role of a prostitute, God plays the role of a faithful husband. Even though we will never be perfect, Ephesians 5:25 calls husbands to love as Jesus loves. "Husbands, love your wives, as Christ loved the church and gave himself up for her." Make a fundamental commitment never to separate what God joins together (see Mark 10:9). God calls you to be a Hosea even if you marry a Gomer (see Hosea 2:14–3:1). This is risky romance filled deep with sacrifice.

Wedding vows are weighty and are made before a holy God. Our yes must be yes, and our no must be no (see Matt. 5:37). If there is any potential exit plan from marriage in your mind, then you must include it in your vows or completely leave off the phrase "till death do us part." You can't have it both ways. Ask the Holy Spirit for grace to help you write your vows in concrete instead of with a dry-erase marker.

We all long for something to last a lifetime. We love it when the Psalmist repeats the phrase "[the LORD's] steadfast love endures forever" (Ps. 106:1). Those statements calm our hearts and cause us to worship.

I am praying for you as you prepare for the weighty thrill of covenanting together with your bride. May your marriage oaths be true until either you or the heavens and earth pass away.

Until then,
Sean

DISCUSSION QUESTIONS

1. Is there anything your partner could do that would make you pursue divorce? If so, what is it and why?
2. Are you willing to make a commitment before God and others to never divorce each other? Why or why not?

SHOULD WE END
OUR ENGAGEMENT?

Sean

Dear Romantic,

No one enters an engagement with the goal of ending it without wedding bells. Yet here you are. Your stomach is turning into knots, and it *isn't* because you are excited. You are wondering if you should bring your engagement to an end.

I mentioned in the previous letter that marriage is meant to be permanent. I spoke about the weight of your future wedding vows and about letting your yes be yes. You probably thought your engagement would end with an exchange of vows, but now you are wondering if you should call the whole thing off before it is too late. Is it is wrong to break off an engagement? Are there good reasons to call off a wedding? How would a person know if it is best not to move forward?

The Bible doesn't have a specific term for the Western phenomenon we call engagement. Engagements did not take place when the Bible was written. Arranged marriages can be found in the Old Testament, and betrothals are mentioned a few times in the New Testament. However, both of these relationship categories are different from what is commonly called engagement. Couples in arranged marriages didn't have to deliberate whether or not to call things off, because it was already decided for them! Ending a betrothal was possible, but it was much more intense than ending an engagement. To break a betrothal required a certificate of divorce (see Matt. 1:18–19).

Although the Bible doesn't discuss engagement, it doesn't leave us stranded in the dark either. The Scriptures are relevant and are always ready to help us honor Christ in every circumstance. I don't know your specific situation, but at least two biblical categories come to mind that warrant breaking an engagement. These categories include unknown factors and rash words.

UNKNOWN FACTORS

When a couple enters an engagement, they are *not* entering a covenantal relationship. Marriage is a covenant before God that only God himself should break (see Mark 10:9). Marriage is a commitment "to have and to hold" until "death do us part." Covenantal vows are not exchanged, however, when a couple gets engaged.

Engagement is a commitment to marry, but it is not an unconditional commitment. When a man drops the knee and proposes to a woman, he is proposing to the woman he *knows*. When a woman says yes to a man, she is saying yes to the man she believes him to be. Each person is agreeing to marry a sinner, but both are agreeing to marry the sinner they know.

Facts can surface during an engagement that were previously unknown. Unfortunately, some people wait until engagement to reveal secret sin that was hidden during the season of dating. (See Sean Perron and Spencer Harmon, *Letters to a Romantic: On Dating* [Phillipsburg: NJ, 2017], chaps. 10, 15, and 16, to read about when and how to have these difficult conversations.) These sins can include a variety of vices but are typically sexual in nature. If a partner reveals current secret sins, such as pornography, fornication, or homosexuality, it changes the understanding on which the engagement was based. It is not fair or loving for a person to propose (or to accept a proposal) while not being forthright about significant areas of his or her soul.

Love of neighbor requires couples to be honest, genuine, and transparent before entering into a lifelong covenant of marriage (see Rom. 12:9). When previously unknown facts emerge that are serious and concerning, it is best to place an engagement on pause until you can achieve full clarity.

If you have discovered new information about your partner that is troubling you, now is the time to talk through these things and receive godly counsel. If you have been hiding facts or have not been fully transparent about an important matter, now is the time to truly love your partner and come clean.

RASH WORDS

Proposing or accepting a proposal isn't like saying yes to fries with your burger. We have all done it when standing in line at a fast-food restaurant. Hunger sets in, the line is getting longer, and the man behind the register asks if you'd like to upgrade your entrée to a meal combo. You stutter, stumble, think about your budget or your diet for two seconds, and then commit. "Sure, why not?" The heat of the moment can contribute to a rash decision that wasn't planned or calculated.

Some engagements are ordered fast-food style. The feelings

were fun, the moment felt fuzzy, and your partner's eyes seemed to sparkle. But reality and logic were not present.

When the emotional buzz subsides, a rash commitment becomes terrifying (see Judg. 11:35). If you find yourself caught in a situation in which you realize you don't truly love the person you are engaged to marry, now is the time to reassess. Or if you have just discovered that you are unprepared for marriage and are worried about making a bad decision, reach out for help. Don't be afraid to call a wiser and more mature Christian and explain what you are feeling to them.

ENDING WELL DOESN'T
REQUIRE WEDDING BELLS

Ending an engagement can be brutal and embarrassing. It may be one of the most difficult things you will ever encounter in life. The thought of calling off a wedding may leave you feeling petrified. But I want to assure you of this: it is not too late to do the right thing. You have not reached the point of no return.

Depending on your situation, the most loving thing you can do for your partner may be to call off the wedding. It is better to remain single than to marry the wrong person. Two wrongs don't make a right. It is better to repent and ask for forgiveness than to follow through with a rash and irresponsible commitment. Ending well doesn't require wedding bells. Don't keep all these thoughts in your head; call a trusted and godly counselor today, and let them share your burdens.

Until then,
Sean

DISCUSSION QUESTIONS

1. Are you having second thoughts about getting married to your partner? Do you know someone who is wise and godly whom you can talk to about this today?
2. Did you make a decision to enter engagement too quickly? Have new facts about your partner been revealed that change your view of him or her?
3. Are there any secret sins that you have not revealed to each other?

MAKING DECISIONS TOGETHER

Sean

Dear Romantic,

On a personal note, I don't need to remind many people that there is very little reason for my wife to be thrilled about me. I'm not all that and a bag of chips. Yet my smallest accomplishments earn the same applause from my wife as if I were awarded a Nobel Peace Prize. If I fix a bolt on an old piece of furniture, I'm MacGyver. If I make a layup on the court while competing against the nine-year-olds we babysit, I'm LeBron James. If I demolish a wasps' nest, I surpass Jason Bourne. She bubbles over with enthusiasm for whatever my hands find to do.

But she is more than a cheerleader. She is an essential part of my life and ministry. Jenny is my sister in Christ just as much as she is my wife. There have been many wonderful times when her gentle rebuke has set me back on course. I can't tell you how many times she has encouraged me in the faith and held up my weary hands.

And if that weren't enough, she blossoms beautifully in submission. If I ask Jenny about moving to another state and starting a ministry from the ground up, she will be "in it to win it." She will have questions, we will discuss it, and she will want to know what our pastors think, but ultimately she will submit to my leadership. She is a helper extraordinaire (see Gen. 2:18–20).

Why do I say all this? Because my wife rejoices in her God-given role as my wife. She is not oppressed. Jenny loves being a woman. In her own words, "Submission is a gift to be embraced. You live the good life by embodying the role God designed." She is thrilled to be a helpmate. She is humble, submissive, gentle, compassionate, and obedient to God. The reason she thinks I am awesome is not because I am. She thinks I'm the best husband in the world because she is the best wife in the world.

MANSIONS TO DECORATE

God has given men and women different roles in marriage. We are both equal and beautiful in God's image, and yet we have different functions. The man is called to lead, guide, and protect his wife. The woman is called to honor, follow, and submit to her husband (see Eph. 5:22–33).

The roles God designed for us are not prisons to escape from but mansions to decorate. God's roles for men and women are not putrid veggies to swallow; they are the choicest meats to feast upon. God created us to flourish and thrive in the gender role he sovereignly bestowed upon each of us.

The husband is not to be a dictator or tyrant. Men are called to be like Jesus—and Jesus is a shepherd (see Ps. 23). Shepherds don't beat their sheep. They protect them from wolves and clean off their thistles. Shepherds care for their flocks and lead them beside still waters. In the same way, husbands are to wash their wives through the water of the Word and pursue them with goodness and mercy all the days of their lives (see Eph. 5:26).

Biblical headship is a weighty responsibility. In Ephesians 5:25, a husband is called to love like Christ. This tall order should cause husbands to tremble humbly before the holy God of the gospel. Husbands are called to lay down their lives, their preferences, their wishes, and their selfish ambitions for their brides. Jesus lived out this love and proved John 15:13 true: "Greater love has no one than this, that someone lay down his life for his friends."

WHAT DOES THIS LOOK LIKE PRACTICALLY?

A husband and wife will discuss and dialogue about all kinds of decisions during a typical week. Most of the decisions we make on a daily basis are based on preference, not on right or wrong. When it comes to preference, Christians are called to consider others above themselves (see Phil. 2:3). If your spouse wants to eat tacos instead of burgers, why not go with his or her preference? If your spouse wants to watch a movie instead of read a book, why not? If they want to take the interstate instead of back roads, why not take it? Our preferences are not the precepts of the Lord. The goal is to outdo one another in kindness (see Rom. 12:10). Love leads with sacrifice, and this produces a joyful home.

There are also significant decisions about jobs, churches, family crises, and so on that shape a family. The husband is to lead by listening. It is important for a husband to truly understand his wife and consider any objections she may have. The channels of conversation and prayer must be open and cleared of any sin. "Likewise, husbands, live with your wives in an understanding way, showing honor to the woman as the weaker vessel, since they are heirs with you of the grace of life, so that your prayers may not be hindered" (1 Peter 3:7).

After an issue is lovingly addressed, the husband has the final call in the matter. The wife is called to submit to the leadership of her husband and to trust that God has given him authority and wisdom over the home. "Now as the church submits to Christ, so also wives should submit in everything to their husbands" (Eph. 5:24).

Biblical submission is a relieving reality for a wife. A wife must believe that God has given her husband authority to lead the home and that she can submit to him. She can experience relief and safety as she submits in faith. The pressure is off. This is a mysterious experience that causes the world to gasp and look at the glorious picture of Christ and his bride.

Adopting this view of life affects everything. When Jenny and I were engaged, our counselors wisely encouraged us to go ahead and determine which of us would be responsible for certain everyday tasks in the home. Who was going to do the dishes? Who would take out the trash and mow the yard? Who would be responsible for keeping track of the finances? Who would make dinner?

Don't wait until marriage to begin cultivating these characteristics. As you consider this season of your relationship, think of ways you can begin to lead and submit. This will look different for each of you. Here are a couple of examples:

Future husband, gently protect your future bride from all the unnecessary demands and expectations placed on her during this busy season. Give up any silly preferences that you have for the wedding and honeymoon. Seek to serve her, and don't be detached from the planning. Leaders are intentional and selfless. Ask yourself where you can tenderly lead her.

Future wife, humbly allow your groom to take the lead in decision-making. Voice your opinions in a way that respects him and speaks the truth in love. Trust his judgment, and free your-self from the pressure of making the final call. Ask yourself in what ways you can lovingly submit to him.

My wife was committed to these biblical principles before we got married. She was blooming beautifully then and is flour-ishing now. I can't get enough of her. It is my prayer that as a cou-ple your headship and submission would stir your affections for each other and attract people to the God of this glorious gospel.

Are you ready to rejoice in your gender roles for God's glory?

Until then,
Sean

DISCUSSION QUESTIONS

1. Are you hesitant about following the particular gender role that God has assigned to you? Why or why not?
2. Make a list of all the current responsibilities you and your partner have as you prepare for the wedding day. See how you can serve each other by taking responsibility for these tasks.
3. Make a list of jobs and responsibilities that will arise in marriage, and designate who will typically be responsible for those tasks.
4. For further reading, see Stuart Scott's *The Exemplary Hus-band* (Bemidji, MN: Focus Publishing, 2002) and Martha Peace's *The Excellent Wife* (Bemidji, MN: Focus Publish-ing, 1999).

CHOOSING A CHURCH

Spencer

Dear Romantic,

Merging your life with your future spouse is delightful and difficult. It feels fitting to intertwine your life with your partner as you prepare for marriage, and God designed it to be that way. But in a fallen world, tying the loose ends of your life together with a fellow sinner can be painful. And, as I'm sure you have noticed, many of the conversations that happen in this season are less about what is right and wrong and more about what is wise and best for *your* marriage.

One particularly difficult challenge is choosing a church. Some couples have the joy of already being members of the same church as they enter marriage, making this decision automatic and easy. Perhaps this is not your situation. Maybe you both love your own churches, have deep relationships in those communities, and serve there regularly. Both of you may believe that staying in your own church would be best for your marriage. Entering into the new season of marriage is enough of a change already without the thought of transitioning to another church too.

The local church should be the central hub of your spiritual life, and the community you commit to will deeply impact your marriage and family for decades. This is no small decision, and it is good to handle it with care. There are so many unique factors involved in your particular situation that there is no way to address them all here. However, as you have these conversations together, make sure that you keep these categories in mind.

START WITH *YOUR* HEART

Before you were engaged, finding a local church was relatively simple. Sure, maybe you struggled with where you could best serve or wanted to know more about the church's stance on a particular topic. But the main thing you were considering was how *you* could serve *your* church. You wanted to know if *you* fit well in this community.

Enter engagement.

Suddenly, *you* are not the only person in the equation when it comes to your decisions. You begin to adopt a *one-flesh mindset*. God calls you to put your fiancé's needs above your own. Their concerns must be your concerns, and the decision about which local church to attend is not simply *your* decision anymore. So, before any conversation with each other, any visiting of churches, any conversations with church leaders, fill your heart with the posture and priorities of Scripture.

The posture of Scripture is to put on compassionate hearts filled with "kindness, humility, meekness, and patience" (see Col. 3:12–14). As your future spouse visits your church and maybe even shares concerns about it, are you prideful and defensive or open and humble? God wants you to have a tender heart and a humble mind (see 1 Peter 3:8).

Scripture's priorities for the church must also fill your heart.

Resolve now to look for evidences of grace in your partner's church as you visit, rather than simply comparing it to your own church. If your partner's church is faithfully preaching God's Word (see 2 Tim. 4:2), caring for its members (see 1 Peter 5:2), and eagerly proclaiming the gospel to the world (see Matt. 28:18–20), rejoice and thank God. Fill your heart with Scripture's priorities for the church, and be delighted when you see your fiancé's church seeking those priorities.

PREFERENCES AND PERSPECTIVES

Understanding the priorities of Scripture keeps you from confusing them with your personal preferences. If your heart is full of humility and with God's priorities for his church as defined by his Word, you won't idolize your preferences. The members of your partner's church might dress more formally than you're used to but also be faithfully pursuing the local community. Your church might use different instruments than your partner's church, but both churches' songs are centered on Christ and faithful to Scripture. These preferences are important, but they are not nonnegotiable. To elevate the way that members dress or the instruments used during worship to the level of a deal breaker is to confuse your personal preferences with biblical priorities.

Let your future spouse's preferences be a sharpening perspective rather than a threat. No local church is perfect, and your partner's preferences might expose weaknesses in your own church that you never noticed before. Perhaps your church lacks age or ethnic diversity. Perhaps your church could be more faithful to share the gospel with the community around them. These are opportunities to see the burdens that God has given your future spouse.

CONCLUDE WITH YOUR ROLES

As you fill your heart with the posture and priorities of Scripture and study the preferences of your future spouse, how do you ultimately make this decision about your church? The best way to make it is within the unique role that God has given you in your marriage.

Men, you should take responsibility for making an understanding, sacrificial decision for the good of your entire family. Since this is a decision that will affect your family after marriage, it is an area in which you are called to lead your *future* wife. This does *not* mean that you as a couple will automatically go to your church. Often it means that you choose to lead your family to your future wife's church, so that your wife can flourish spiritually as she transitions into marriage. It's your responsibility to live with your wife in a considerate way (see 1 Peter 3:7). Men, do you know the things that your fiancée values in a local church? Do you know her spiritual gifts? Have you talked with her about where she will thrive most and why?

Ladies, you should take responsibility for joyfully submitting to the leadership of your future husband. This is a unique opportunity for you to trust the leadership of the man you have promised to follow for the rest of your days. Allow your fiancé to lead your relationship spiritually in this first major decision of your future marriage. Be honest and open with him about your concerns and questions. Don't conceal any distractions or obstacles that will keep you from worshipping at a particular church. Encourage him to prioritize what Scripture says is most important in the local church. When he makes his decision, joyfully submit to his leadership, trusting that he is seeking the good of your new family in what he decides.

YOUR NEW CHURCH

Whatever church you commit to will be new—whether it is yours, your partner's, or a completely different church. It will be new because, once you are married, a new family will be created. Your new family will be worshipping Christ together, serving together, and being discipled together. Each of you will have a different perspective on your local church as you share in community together.

But, although many things will be new, some things won't change. You worship the same God, the same Spirit indwells these church members, and you still have the same mission. May you make this decision for the sake of that God, by the power of that Spirit, and for the sake of that mission.

Until then,
Spencer

DISCUSSION QUESTIONS

1. What are your nonnegotiables for a local church? Are they biblical priorities or personal preferences?
2. What are some ways you would like to serve together as a married couple? What are your gifts as a couple?
3. Do you have any concerns about your partner's church? What are they?

A SPIRITUAL RELATIONSHIP

Sean

Dear Romantic,

When I hit middle school, I became enamored with the idea of a girlfriend. I discovered the possibility of a "relationship" that was charged with romance. It was also during this season that I became interested in the Bible. My parents had shared many Bible stories with me, but I had never explored the Scriptures for myself. I attended church often and claimed Christ by affiliation, but I held an uncracked Bible in hand every Sunday.

At the right moment, someone at church asked me a series of questions about my desire to have a girlfriend. He asked whether someone would date me if I spent only one hour a week with her. He wanted to know how long my girlfriend would last if I spent only ten minutes a day talking to her. I scoffed as I thought about a romantic relationship that could be sustained with only a ten-minute conversation each day. I didn't know much, but I knew that dating for one hour a week was a recipe for a breakup.

My friend then stunned me by asking me why I thought I had a relationship with God when I spent only a few hours a week in church. He asked me how much time I dedicated to meeting Jesus in the Bible. I couldn't answer him. I had never thought about my affiliation with Jesus in terms of an actual relationship. I realized that I barely knew the God I claimed to love.

Don't get me wrong—relationships are not sustained by time clocks. You don't punch in hours with your girlfriend, fiancé, or spouse. That sounds miserable. Relationships are built off of delight and commitment.

Do you remember the long phone calls with your partner when you were dating? You talked (in between giggles) about nothing into the wee hours of the night. Do you recall all the energy you placed into writing handwritten notes or racking your brain for new date ideas while trying to keep a running list of his or her favorite things? All this happened because your heart was filled with love. Love drove your hard work.

It is no secret that relationships take effort, but we forget this when we are in the heat of the moment. When romantic feelings are surging through your system, you aren't counting your hours of energy. Delight drives your discipline, and you are willing to go the extra mile for the one you love.

The same should be true of your relationship with Christ. Are you filled with joy for God? Does this drive you to be disciplined and to cultivate habits of worship? Don't believe the lie that you will be super spiritual after you are married. Don't think that your big sins will simply become small sins later. Marriage is not a magic wand for making sin disappear. Spiritual maturity is hard work that begins now. Exchanging marriage vows is not a spiritual energy drink that suddenly makes you godly.

It is not an overstatement to say that the joy of your marriage will depend on your delight in God. Delight in God is furthered by meditation on the Bible (see Ps. 119:47). Take a few minutes to ask yourself this: How significant is Scripture to you and your future spouse? Is it noticeably important? Do you change your patterns of life in order to meditate on it?

Let Psalm 1 direct your romantic relationship: "Blessed is the man who walks not in the counsel of the wicked . . . but his delight is in the law of the LORD, and on his law he meditates day and night" (vv. 1–2).

Future husbands, how will you lead your bride into the Scriptures? How will you wash her daily with the Word? What is your plan? What rhythms are you embedding now that will enable you to dance in the days ahead? You won't become her spiritual authority until marriage, but that doesn't mean you can't take initiative in leading. Your fiancée needs to know that you will be able to wash her in the Word (see Eph. 5:26).

Future wives, how do you prioritize the Bible in your personal life? Do you have a sustainable Bible-reading plan? Do you think about particular passages of Scripture throughout the day? The more we are in God's Word, the more our prayer lives will be enhanced. The rich blessings of prayer come because God's words abide in us and we in them (see John 15:7).

I want to encourage both of you to begin daily encountering God in his Word. It is important that you do this both separately and together. Some couples follow the same Bible-reading plans in their private devotions and then come together weekly to discuss what they have been studying. I know others who are on different reading schedules but who discuss their personal readings with each other with great frequency. Don Whitney talks about the basics of family worship under the three categories of "read, pray, sing."[1] These three acts do not have to be complicated or drawn out.

---

1. We have been helped greatly by Dr. Don Whitney's writings. See his short and readable book *Family Worship* (Wheaton, IL: Crossway, 2016). I also

As a married couple, Jenny and I try to do these three things each night before bed. Some nights we sing a whole psalm, while other nights we make it through only one stanza. The goal is to create biblical rhythms in your daily life that draw you into the presence of God.

Go ahead and purpose to produce beautiful music in your marriage. Take the time now to get into some rhythms so that you can dance with delight later in marriage.

Until then,
Sean

DISCUSSION QUESTIONS

1. How often do you spend time communing with Jesus during a typical week?
2. How often do you talk about the Bible as a couple?
3. What is your plan to help cultivate spiritual disciplines in your future home?

---

highly recommend his book *Spiritual Disciplines for the Christian Life*, rev. ed. (Colorado Springs: NavPress, 2014).

MAINTAINING FRIENDSHIPS

Spencer

Dear Romantic,

The engagement season feels all-consuming, doesn't it? Somehow it seems that every strand of your life ties back to the wedding day. You and your future spouse might both be working extra hours to save for your honeymoon. At work, everyone is asking you, "How many more days?" You are addressing invitations and have even spent a few date nights registering for gifts.

The busyness of life during the season of engagement can make it difficult to maintain friendships with those who are not directly linked to your wedding day. You know that your friends love you, but you don't want to neglect them during this season of your life. You want to serve them and spend time with them.

Although you have this desire, it's easy to get so consumed in the details of your wedding that you forget about your non-engaged friends. It's difficult to balance between wedding plans and other relationships in such a busy season of life, but consider taking these few steps to encourage your friendships over the next months.

YOUR CONSISTENT EAR

Things are beginning to change in your friendships. Your belongings are slowly moving into boxes in your apartment. Traditional hangout nights with friends are being replaced with wedding-planning sessions with your fiancé. You're working more than ever before to save money. You are taking on more responsibility and commitment than ever before, and your friendships must accommodate.

Relationships are made up of moments and presence. One of the best ways you can serve your single friends during this time is to be present with them when you have time together. Although your time is limited, be slow to speak and quick to hear during the time that you do have (see Prov. 10:19). Make it your aim to ask questions of your friends when you are together so you can stay connected. Try to make each moment count. Are there trials that your friends are walking through? Are there new opportunities they are considering? What is God teaching them right now?

THEIR CONSISTENT WORD

Married people are not the only ones who can relate to your burdens during engagement. You probably feel a pull to spend more time with people who are in the same season of life as you. Although it is a good thing to spend time with those who understand your experiences, don't discount the impact that your unmarried friends can have on your engagement. Scripture paints a picture of the church as those who speak the truth in love to one another so that all believers will be built up in love (see Eph. 4:15–16). All believers are qualified to speak the truth in love and to bear the burdens of others (Gal. 6:2). Are you allowing your unmarried friends to have a voice in your life during your engagement, or are you limiting your relationships to those who are in the same season of life as you?

Married or single, engaged or dating, each Christian is indwelt by the Holy Spirit. This Spirit gives believers unique gifts so that they can bless the church. All believers are given a "manifestation of the Spirit for the common good" (1 Cor. 12:7). On top of this, all believers are members of one body, and no member can say to another, "I have no need of you" (1 Cor. 12:21). It dishonors the Holy Spirit to act as though your unmarried friends have nothing to contribute to this season of your life.

There are unique ways in which your unmarried friends can minister to you. Are there spiritual gifts you know they have that you do not have? Gifts of service, leadership, and exhortation (Rom. 12:6–8) are needed as engaged couples plan their weddings. Let your single friends serve and minister to you as you enter this new season of life.

There are unique challenges that arise during your engagement. As they do, communicate them to your single friends so they can pray for you and encourage you from God's Word. Bearing one another's burdens in love is one of the main ways that God knits our hearts together as the body of Christ. Do not keep this precious gift from your single friends.

YOUR MANY-MEMBERED FAMILY

As a member of Christ's body, you are called to serve and be served by those who are different from you: Latino, black, Asian, white, male, female, married, single, rich, poor. The glory of God's church is that it is composed of many members, and your single friends are a part of this many-membered family.

Consider them members of the same family as you—because they are. You are meant to mutually carry one another's burdens, be encouraged by one another's faith, and be helped by one another's gifts. You have been baptized into the same Spirit, and that Spirit will continue to use your single friends in your life as you love, listen to, and minister to one another.

Until then,
Spencer

DISCUSSION QUESTIONS

1. What burdens could you share with your friends during this season?
2. How can you include your friends and their spiritual gifts in your current season of life?

LOVING YOUR NEW PARENTS

Spencer

Dear Romantic,

Some of our strangest quirks surface only around family. We see our idiosyncrasies in those strange family traditions, in the family debate around the dinner table, or in our reaction to the sibling who can frustrate us like no one else. Our families often reveal aspects of ourselves that bloom only through familiarity, time, and comfort.

Currently your head is swirling with the idea of welcoming another family into your life. While it's refreshing to see the inner workings of another family, you've already noticed those oddities of your partner's family that seem so normal to them but strange to you. On top of this, someone recently told you the old adage, "When you marry your spouse, you marry their family." While you love your soon-to-be family, the idea of *marrying* them sounds strange and a little unnerving.

It's understandable that people say things like this, but it is mistaken. You are *not* marrying your future spouse's family. You are making a covenant with *your wife*—not her family—when you marry. Scripture teaches that when two people marry, they each leave their father and mother and hold fast to their spouse (Gen. 2:24). This is an exclusive covenant between you and your wife that neither of your parents makes with you.

Yet it's important for you to recognize that, although you are beginning a new family, you are simultaneously joining another one. Your future spouse represents a heritage and an investment made by his or her parents over decades. In a very real way, you are the newcomer. Your future spouse's parents have loved, cared for, and cherished your fiancé before you knew that he or she existed. Your partner will always be fundamentally connected to his or her parents, and thus you will too. It's important, then, for you to consider how to love both of your families while also leaving both of your families.

HONOR THE INVESTMENT

Your future spouse represents thousands of conversations, countless hours, and a lifetime of deep affection from his or her parents. Even if your partner comes from a complex family situation, his or her parents still brought your partner into the world and chose to raise him or her. The care, love, pain, and knowledge of your partner that they have should be honored, not spited, by you. Future in-laws are not a burden to be carried; nor are they a nuisance to be endured. They are the guardians of a treasure you are about to receive. They should be honored as such, and the gravity of their investment—no matter how small—should inform your thoughts and attitude toward them.

One temptation that you might experience as you transition into marriage is to exclude your in-laws as a statement of your independence. Couples oftentimes bankrupt themselves of wisdom, insight, and experience because they are committed to *leaving* but not to *loving*. Excluding your in-laws from your life, decisions, and plans during engagement, however, is not independence—it's isolation. Isolation typically indicates self-ishness (see Prov. 18:1), and now is the time for you to cultivate a servant mind-set in your marriage. This does not mean that your in-laws get the final say in your home. However, recognizing their investment means *including* them in your relationship. Remember that they have known your future spouse much longer than you have. They can be your dearest counselors as you consider how to serve your spouse in this new season of marriage.

CONTINUE THE INVESTMENT

Your in-laws are not a means to an end. They are not a test that you pass or fail in order to graduate into marriage. Rather, they represent an important relationship that will be central in your life for years to come. Instead of pulling away from your in-laws, draw near to them. Consider sitting down with your fiancé's parents and asking them how to best serve their son or daughter as you move into marriage with him or her. Ask for advice, ideas, and ways you can serve your partner as a spouse. Even if your in-laws have a track record of not caring for your spouse, this demonstrates humility in your relationship with your in-laws that will show them the humility of Christ (see Phil. 2:5–11).

Find some way to allow your in-laws to invest in you. This does not need to be spiritual investment. It could be wisdom with finances, help in decorating your home, practical tips on fixing household items, or advice for an upcoming decision. Allow your in-laws to continue investing in both their son or daughter and you—even in a small way.

RECOGNIZE BOUNDARIES

Although your in-laws represent years of investment in your future spouse, a decisive change must be recognized between your partner and his or her parents. Your relationship with your in-laws will not thrive if this changing relationship is not recognized and communicated. Instead, bitterness will grow as unspoken expectations are not met.

As you prepare for marriage, decide together what boundaries would be appropriate between you and your families. This conversation might involve the frequency of visits home, dynamics in each other's families, or the type of influence your families will have on your marriage. Gathering insight from a trusted married friend can get you and your fiancé on the same page before communicating with your families.

As you decide what your family will look like, communicate these boundaries to your families in kindness and at appropriate times. Listen to your in-laws, understand their desires, and communicate the priorities of your newly forming family. Consider this as an act of love, not a declaration of independence. You are seeking to love your in-laws in order to have a growing, loving relationship with them.

WHEN THERE IS NO INVESTMENT

As some of you read this, your heart aches. This chapter is unrealistic for you because one or both sets of your parents haven't made an investment in you and your partner. Therefore there is no investment to honor or continue. Perhaps you have no way of knowing your future in-laws, or perhaps they have neglected your partner. How do you love them?

First, although the pattern of Scripture is for parents to

invest in their children (see Prov. 1:8; 23:22; Eph. 6:1–4), the beauty of the church is that it becomes a family for those who have none. When we are adopted into God's family, we receive fathers, mothers, brothers, and sisters in the faith (see Mark 10:29–30; Eph. 2:19; 1 Tim. 5:1-2). Allow the local church to fulfill God's purpose in your life by becoming a family for you and your future spouse.

Second, seek to live at peace with your in-laws. Although you can't control your in-laws' desire to be a part of your relationship, you can seek to love them in tangible ways so that you express your desire for a peaceful relationship with them. Call them to update them on wedding plans, invite them to the wedding, and pray for them.

Third, commit to forgiveness over the long haul. Perhaps your in-laws have deeply hurt you or your partner. Even though you are seeking to live peaceably with all (see Rom. 12:18), it might not be possible for your relatives to be fully reconciled with you before the wedding day. Instead, entrust this relationship to God and commit with your partner to prayer, peace, and tangible expression of love over the years. Do not be overcome with any evil that your in-laws have done to you or your partner, but overcome evil with good (see Rom. 12:21).

COVENANTING IN LOVE

Although you are not marrying your in-laws, commit to loving them. Be at peace with them. Move toward them in honor and conversation. And, as you love them, view your relationship as something that is intended to bless both you and them for years to come. The pattern of Scripture is for the older to invest in the younger (see Titus 2:3–5) and for parents to teach and train their children (see Prov. 1:8; 23:22). The cumulative effect of honoring your families will result in the sweetness of unity and in access to some of the best counselors. Love while leaving.

Until then,
Spencer

DISCUSSION QUESTIONS

1. How are you currently honoring your families during your engagement?
2. In what ways do your future in-laws know your future spouse better than you?
3. How is loving your in-laws difficult for you? How does God's Word address this difficulty?

SHOULD WE ELOPE?

Spencer

Dear Romantic,

In the grand scheme of things, engagement is not long; however, when you are engaged, the season can seem just a little shorter than an eternity. As if the sheer waiting were not enough, you feel pressure on all sides. Wedding planning, striving for purity, pre-marriage counseling—all of this in preparation for the big day and every day after that. Engagement is not long, but it seems daunting to carry a burden that feels heavier every day.

During this time, it's tempting to toy with the idea of eloping. Not "disappear to Las Vegas and hire Elvis to marry you" eloping, but cancelling your wedding plans, going to the courthouse, and privately covenanting to one another. At this point in the game, it seems like a delight simply to be united to your spouse without the stress of planning the wedding. It's still early in your wedding planning; you haven't sent out invitations—wouldn't it be easier to just say no to the pomp and circumstance of a wedding? Does it really matter?

Eloping isn't always a bad idea, and there are certain complex situations in which it may be the best option. But before you make a decision this significant, you need to take some time with your future spouse to consider what you are giving up and gaining if you decide to elope.

The problem with most couples' desire to elope is that it is typically motivated by relief rather than reason. "Desire without knowledge is not good, and whoever makes haste with his feet misses his way," says Proverbs 19:2. The pressures you are currently experiencing are certainly *real*, but that does not mean it is *right* to make a fast decision for quick relief. Before you make a significant decision like this, you need to slow down, not speed up.

SANCTIFICATION

A season of waiting and pressure is sometimes the will of God for our lives. Paul calls us to rejoice in our sufferings (see Rom. 5:3–5), and James tells us that we should let the steadfastness brought about by waiting through suffering have its full effect in our lives (see James 1:4). Although it is "better to marry than to burn with passion" (1 Cor. 7:9), that does not mean that this period of engagement is your enemy. If you are running from engagement because it is difficult or because eloping would be easier, you should check your heart. You could be running from a means of sanctification in your life.

Whether it is sexual temptation, financial feasibility, family tension, or a life situation, ask yourself this before you make the decision: are we running from an opportunity for sanctification? God often refines us through the waiting (see Ps. 62:5–8).

SERVICE

One of my biggest concerns with eloping is that it can often be motivated by selfishness rather than service: *your* purity has been tested, *your* stress level is high, *you* are concerned about *your* finances, *you* are tired of planning *your* wedding. The common denominator in all these problems is your concerns, your feelings, and your situation. Although those concerns are legitimate, your reasons are void of other people.

The distinct mark of mature decision-making is that it considers how the decision will affect not only you but also everyone around you. More than that, the distinct mark of mature Christian decision-making is thinking of others as more significant than yourself. "Let each of you look not only to his own interests, but also to the interests of others" (Phil. 2:4). Have you thought about how a decision like this would affect both of your families? One of the great benefits of a wedding is that it provides an opportunity to recognize and honor those who have invested their lives into shaping you and your spouse as individuals. Your parents, extended family, friends, fellow church members—all of them have played a significant role in your life and relationship. Will it serve them, or only you, to elope?

OPPORTUNITY

Weddings provide once-in-a-lifetime opportunities to share Christ with those who do not know him. Consider this: your wedding is probably the one church-related event that non-Christian people will desire to attend and at which you will have control over the details. In the midst of all the stress of planning, have you thought about the purpose of the planning? The fragrance of the gospel could fill the ceremony for all your family and friends to sense. Have you considered the creative ways you could proclaim the gospel throughout the details of your day? The gospel could be preached by your pastor, songs could be sung that glorify Christ, and Scripture could be read that lifts up the meaning of marriage.

Your wedding is not just the occasion of your marriage; it could also be the time for a clear, bold, and winsome presentation of the gospel in word and in deed.

KNOWLEDGE AND LOVE

Desire without knowledge is not good. My main goal in writing this to you is *not* to convince you to have a large, grandiose wedding filled with excess and endless detail. You don't need a large venue, a big wedding party, and the perfect décor in order to proclaim the gospel and honor your family. I am, however, encouraging you to consider the consequences of eloping. I would hate for you to make haste with your feet and then see that you have missed your way.

Slow down, think through the details, consider the possibilities for sanctification, service, and gospel proclamation, and then make your decision. Whatever choice you make, I pray that it is motivated by love and compelled by service.

Until then,
Spencer

DISCUSSION QUESTIONS

1. What will you gain and lose by eloping?
2. Is your desire to elope based primarily on reason or on relief? Why do you think this?

HANDLING CONFLICT

Sean and Jenny

Dear Romantic,

As couples get to know each other, conflict inevitably arises. The great irony is that quarrels can often erupt over the smallest matters. An argument might not seem small in the heat of the moment, but after things cool down you realize that often the smallest coals can burn the hottest.

A helpful question to ask when conflict arises is "Why did we quarrel?" The book of James says that we fight because our pleasures are at war inside us. "What causes quarrels and what causes fights among you? *Is it not this, that your passions are at war within you?* You desire and do not have, so you murder. You covet and cannot obtain, so you fight and quarrel. You do not have, because you do not ask. You ask and do not receive, because you ask wrongly, to spend it on your passions" (James 4:1–3).

I believe that quarrels result when we seek pleasure within ourselves rather than in God and in service to each other. We have our "passions," and these passions are lusts for the things we want but don't have. We want, so we fight to get what we want.

For example, in the Perron home, we have had differing

opinions about time. I am typically slower, and Jenny is frequently faster. I go with the flow while Jenny channels the flow. This has manifested itself when we are running late or behind schedule. Jenny's passion is to arrive on time, while my passion is to arrive "within reason." If these passions take priority, though, they can lead to quarrelling between us.

You might be wondering how selfishness can be at the root of quarreling. But ask yourself this question: "If I had been thinking about how I could love my partner, would I have become so frustrated?" When you are looking for an opportunity to be patient with your future spouse, it is hard to get upset. When you are looking for an opportunity to be gentle, you will be slow to anger.

In our relationship, I can serve Jenny by waking up earlier in order to make the morning smoother. Jenny can be understanding toward me and remember that our relationship is more important than arriving on schedule. By considering each other better than ourselves and outdoing each other in kindness, the tension weakens and the friction fades.

We are not alone in these temptations. Young couples argue over absurd and trite issues. Couples have received marriage counseling over where their furniture should be positioned. These things ought not to be. But before we cast the first cushion at the sofa sinners, let us examine our own hearts.

We are not far from ruining everything. Sin is deceitful. We must be watchful that we do not find ourselves quarreling over insignificant matters. Purpose in your heart to relinquish your own preferences for the sake of your partner. People are more important than preferences. Paul writes about an intense conflict that the Corinthians were encountering.

> To have lawsuits at all with one another is already a defeat
> for you. Why not rather suffer wrong? Why not rather be

defrauded? But you yourselves wrong and defraud—even your own brothers! (1 Cor. 6:7–8)

If it's better to take a monetary hit and endure social loss than to take your brother to court, how much more should you allow your future spouse to have his or her preferences?

Relinquishing preferences does not give you the freedom to keep score. There should be no scorekeeping among spouses. Love keeps no records of wrongs; it "does not insist on its own way" (1 Cor. 13:5). Do not let your future spouse "have their way" as a favor. This is not about your partner's needs or your needs. This is about *our* need to love like Jesus. Do not scratch their back now so that they will scratch yours later. Beware the back-scratching heart. Jesus gave us an example of love that was selfless. His love had no ulterior motive, and neither should ours.

Does your future spouse prefer five people in the bridal party instead of ten? Would it make the other person happy to register for square plates instead of round ones like your mom has? Do you want 800 square feet in your new apartment while your partner wants 1,200?

These questions (and thousands more like them) intersect when two people enter into a relationship. You will work through these types of scenarios for the rest of your marriage, and the best way forward is to put yourself to death today. If you seek your life by losing it, you will find it (see John 12:25).

When two sinners confess and ask for forgiveness before God and each other, they gloriously display the gospel. Cultivate joy by loving your future spouse in all the small things. The goal is unity and peace. Thankfully, peace is a fruit of the spirit that any Christian can produce.

In the words of the apostle Paul,

Put on then, as God's chosen ones, holy and beloved, compassionate hearts, kindness, humility, meekness, and patience, bearing with one another and, if one has a complaint against another, forgiving each other; as the Lord has forgiven you, so you also must forgive. And above all these put on love, which binds everything together in perfect harmony. And let the peace of Christ rule in your hearts, to which indeed you were called in one body. (Col 3:12–15)

Until then,
Sean and Jenny

DISCUSSION QUESTIONS

1. When you are having an argument, do you typically think of the reasons you love your partner? Or do you dwell on their flaws instead?
2. When it comes to wedding details, are you quick to offer your opinion, or do you let your future spouse pick their preferences first?
3. List five reasons that you can be grateful for your partner even when you are not in total agreement.

PLANNING YOUR PARTIES

Spencer

Dear Romantic,

There are so many reasons to be excited for your wedding day. Not only are you going to covenant your life to your spouse, but you also get to do it in the presence of some of your dearest friends. These friends have walked with you through your deepest joys, darkest sorrows, and warmest memories.

Bridal parties have sacred significance. When you select this group, you are choosing your witnesses. These family members and friends are the ones who will witness the covenant you make with your spouse. By asking them to stand beside you, you are asking them to endorse and hold you accountable to the covenant you are making. It's a good thing to consider who you would like these witnesses to be.

Although the people in your bridal party can be your closest friends, it's easy for some of them to have differing convictions from yours. You desire for them to honor the Lord and serve everyone who comes. You want to have a great time with your friends, but you know that some people often view the "final night" as a time for you to sow wild oats before marriage. Sadly, I have been part of weddings whose bachelor or bachelorette party was filled with crude humor and was not meaningful.

SOAKING IN THE MEANING OF MARRIAGE

It's hypocrisy to hold a biblical view of marriage as a sacred covenant before God but then treat it as only a gateway to sex. But this is often what our pre-wedding parties look like. Instead, let the structure of your party highlight the meaning of marriage. As you consider celebrating with your friends and family, choose to do things that reflect all the gifts that marriage brings to us.

Marriage is a place of joy. When John the Baptist spoke of his role in Jesus' mission, he spoke of himself as a member of a bridal party. Reflecting on Jesus being united with his people, he says, "The friend of the bridegroom . . . rejoices greatly at the bridegroom's voice. Therefore this joy of mine is now complete" (John 3:29). Your pre-marriage party should be marked by noticeable joy. Do the things that encourage celebration and rejoicing—feast at the bride or groom's favorite restaurant, laugh about funny memories, enjoy a fun activity. Do whatever would cultivate godly joy and bring the entire party together in celebration of this great moment.

Marriage is a place of worship. Your marriage will be a sacred reflection of the great story of redemption. You and your wife will reflect Jesus' love for his church and the submission of the church to Jesus (Eph. 5:22–33). All of this is done before God and as an act of worship to him. This act of covenant keeping should compel future husbands and wives to seek after God's help. This means that our pre-wedding parties should be events at which prayer is present, Scripture is shared, and testimonies abound. Consider ending your night with the members of your bridal party praying for you and sharing passages that have encouraged them. I promise that this will be a sweet memory for everyone present.

Marriage is a place of intimacy. Maintaining purity doesn't mean you have to shy away from talking about sex during your pre-wedding party. One of the breathtaking joys that the bride and groom will experience is physical intimacy (see Song 4). The sinful world does not have exclusive jurisdiction over sex, and we should not avoid it as a dirty topic. Rather, we should celebrate it as the good gift that it is. As your conscience permits, enjoy a lingerie shower thrown by a good friend or set aside time when a few married men can share advice on how to best serve your wife during the wedding night. Celebrate sex as a pure and holy gift—not as something designed for crude jokes. As you celebrate this reality, ensure that the people present are already married, so that singles are not tempted to sinful lust from hearing these conversations.

EXPLAINING AND HONORING

Honor your friends and be filled with gratitude that they would seek to celebrate your marriage in this way. As you move closer to your wedding day, communicate up front with bridal party members about your priorities for the night. Tell them clearly the things you want to *avoid* and the things you want to do. You obviously should not plan your own party, but it honors your friends to know how to best serve and celebrate you.

The pre-wedding party is a time for reflecting on the meaning of marriage. And if those who attend do not know its design or the One who designed it, it will be an opportunity for them to see clearly the joys of this covenant and the One whom it reflects.

Until then,
Spencer

DISCUSSION QUESTIONS

1. What are some things you would like to avoid at your bachelor or bachelorette party? What would you like to do instead?
2. Is there a like-minded friend in your party to whom you can communicate these things?

ON MODESTY

Spencer and Taylor

Dear Sister,

Shopping for a dress is stressful. Not only are you trying to find a dress that you actually like, but it really does take extra effort to find something that meets the needs of your wedding and is also modest. You live in a culture that finds its identity in autonomy. You are told you should be able to dress however you want and show off whatever you want.

There are unique complexities for each woman, which we know can be difficult. Taylor and I want to write to you as a brother and sister in Christ and encourage you to glorify God with your body on your wedding day. There are many pressures and many voices that may ask you to compromise. Consider this letter an encouragement and an affirmation of your desire to honor Christ on your wedding day—particularly in the area of modesty.

WHOSE DAY IS IT?

Before you ask another question about how much a dress should cover, how low a neckline should be, or how tight a dress should fit, ask yourself this question: what is the purpose of my wedding day? While this may sound different from what you have been hearing, this is not *your* big day. It's certainly an important and special day. But this day is not yours. Like every other day for every other Christian, this day belongs to Christ. His priorities, values, and glory must soak into our hearts and bleed out in our decisions. You can resolve many complex questions regarding the dos and don'ts of your wedding by asking whether each decision draws attention to or away from the person of Jesus Christ. Whatever you do, do it for the glory of Christ (see 1 Cor. 10:31).

God cares about what we do with our bodies. He actually goes so far as to say that he has bought them with a price—the blood of his Son (see 1 Cor. 6:20). God bought our bodies to be employed in the great enterprise of glorifying his Son. This means that the way you eat, drink, talk, and even dress should be governed by him. Our bodies belong to our kind and wise Father, and he calls us to joyfully respond to his priorities on our wedding day—even in how we dress. God wants us to choose clothing for the wedding day that will highlight the content of our souls rather than the shape of our bodies. Immodesty certainly does not deplete the ceremony of all meaning, but it can distract the audience.

START AT THE END

Envision the end of your wedding. You walk out of the chapel arm in arm with your groom. The crowd then files out the middle aisle. What do you want them to say? What thoughts do you want them to think? Obviously, you can't control everything that is spoken and thought at your wedding. However, you can control some things. You can put intentional effort into ensuring that you highlight the meaning of marriage rather than the form of your body, the precious heart of godliness over your curves. Scripture emphatically states that you should spend more time and attention on your heart than on your appearance (see 1 Peter 3:3–4). What can you do to reflect this value in the way you and your bridesmaids dress?

Please do not think we are saying that you should not care about looking beautiful on your wedding day. Jesus is going to present his bride to himself in radiance and splendor (see Eph. 5:27), and you should radiate and reflect this beauty as you walk down the aisle. Wear attractive makeup, find a beautiful dress, and select gorgeous flowers. What we are saying, however, is that it is possible to diminish the beauty and radiance of this metaphor of Christ and the church when we insert ourselves into the picture. Immodesty says, "Look at me!" while Scripture says, "Look at Christ!"

There are no modesty laws about the length of your dress or the type of gown you choose. Instead, implement a decision filter as you walk through the dress store: will this dress use my body to reflect the meaning of marriage or to distract from it?

REFLECT AND RESOLVE

After you consider what to buy for your wedding day, grab a friend and ask her to think through some questions with you. First, will this dress draw attention to my body in an inappropriate or sexual way? If you believe that it draws attention to your body in a sexual way, resolve not to purchase it. Your body will soon belong to your husband, so why show it off to others before you covenant with him? Second, does this outfit *serve* or *distract* those around me? Love "does not insist on its own way" (1 Cor. 13:5) but always puts the interests of others above its own (see

Phil. 2:4). If your gown has the potential to cause your brothers to stumble, resolve to take it off the list.

Our hearts are filled with gratitude as we consider you diligently searching for the right dress—not just because it is exciting to purchase a dress, but because that search represents something. Remember that shopping for a modest dress is not a duty to drudge through but is worship that pleases your heavenly Father. By putting prayerful thought into how you will adorn yourself, you also give careful attention to how you will wear the gospel.

Until then,
Spencer and Taylor

DISCUSSION QUESTIONS

1. In the core of your being, does it make you happier to draw attention to yourself or to Christ?
2. Is there a godly woman you trust who can help you find a dress that is modest and beautiful?

ON BIRTH CONTROL

Sean and Jenny

Dear Romantic,

As your wedding day approaches, it is completely appropriate for you to begin seeking counsel about contraceptives. There are two major questions you should be asking. First, is it a sin to use contraceptives? Second, if it is not sinful, which contraceptives are permissible to use?

The Bible is abundantly clear that children are a gift from the Lord.

> Behold, children are a heritage from the LORD,
>   the fruit of the womb a reward.
> Like arrows in the hand of a warrior
>   are the children of one's youth.
> Blessed is the man
>   who fills his quiver with them! (Ps. 127:3–5)

In the book of Genesis, God tells his people on two separate occasions to "be fruitful and multiply" (Gen. 1:28; 9:1). This mentality is drastically different from the average Western mindset. Scripture does not see children as a burden. Rather, the Bible views children as a blessing and a delight.

While it is very true that sex is designed to produce children, this is not the only reason that God created sex. Paul talks about sex within marriage in 1 Corinthians 7:5, saying, "Do not deprive one another, except perhaps by agreement for a limited time, that you may devote yourselves to prayer; but then come together again, so that Satan may not tempt you because of your lack of self-control." Biblical ethicists John and Paul Feinberg correctly note that God intended sex as a gift of procreation, companionship, unity, and pleasure as well as a means of curbing fornication and adultery.[1] I'm not convinced that the Bible requires married couples to intend (or even to be willing) to get pregnant each time they have sex. The Scriptures encourage believers to have sex frequently in marriage—and not just when a wife is fertile.

Believers must be very careful not to be selfish in their sexual motives. It is selfish for a couple to use birth control because they do not want the hassle of children. Oftentimes career pursuits, high standards of living, and laziness are the reasons that people use birth control. This, however, does not mean that birth control is intrinsically sinful. Are there acceptable reasons to use discernment about when to have children?

The Bible clearly states that marriage is a good gift from the Lord. "He who finds a wife finds a good thing and obtains favor from the LORD" (Prov. 18:22). "Then the LORD God said, 'It is not good that the man should be alone; I will make him a helper fit for him'" (Gen. 2:18). God has declared marriage good! Why would anyone want to hinder this blessing? According to

---

1. John S. Feinberg and Paul D. Feinberg, *Ethics for a Brave New World*, 2nd ed. (Wheaton, IL: Crossway, 2010), 300–302.

these verses, isn't it immoral for someone to choose to remain single? Well, not necessarily. It all depends on the purpose for staying single.

The apostle Paul writes, "So then he who marries his betrothed does well, and he who refrains from marriage will do even better" (1 Cor. 7:38). Paul argues very effectively that if a believer decides to remain single for the cause of Christ, then it is actually better to avoid the blessing of marriage. I believe this argument is also appropriate for the discussion of birth control.[2]

It is not hard to imagine certain circumstances and seasons in a couple's life that could warrant regulating when and how many children they should have. If a couple is overseas in a hostile or "closed" country on the mission field, it might be better for the advancement of the gospel if they had fewer children. If a couple is very tight on finances or if one spouse is still finishing school, it might be appropriate to exercise wisdom in using birth control. First Timothy 5:8 says, "But if anyone does not provide for his relatives, and especially for members of his household, he has denied the faith and is worse than an unbeliever."

Some believers object, arguing that God should be the one to decide when a wife becomes pregnant. They claim that birth control is sinful because it expresses a lack of faith in God's sovereignty. Let it be clear that God is completely sovereign over conception and the womb (see Ruth 4:13). Nothing happens on earth without God's appointment and permission. However, this does not necessarily mean that birth control is sinful.

In conjunction with his absolute sovereignty, God holds

---

2. This section has been shaped by Piper's writing and thinking on the subject. See John Piper, "Is It Wrong to Use Birth Control?" Desiring God, March 5, 2008, http://www.desiringgod.org/interviews/is-it-wrong-to-use-birth-control.

people responsible for their actions. This is a clear teaching of Scripture that cannot be ignored (see Eccl. 12:13; Rom. 3:19; 9:19–20). It is a fallacy to think that birth control will hinder God's sovereignty. God will not let birth control thwart his eternal plans. He has chosen to give us the mind of Christ and to let us use wisdom and discernment in the cause of advancing his kingdom. This is not contrary to his sovereignty.

While it is true that the Bible says children are a blessing, this does not mean it is ethically necessary to have as many babies as the wife is physically capable of bearing. John Piper has correctly said, "We should make our decisions on Kingdom purposes. If—for Kingdom reasons, gospel reasons, advancement reasons, and radical service reasons—having another child would be unwise then I think we have the right and the freedom to regulate that."[3] The Bible does not forbid birth control as long as it is used selflessly and for the glory of God.

WHAT ABOUT THE PILL?

God alone is the giver and taker of human life (see 1 Sam. 2:6). Scripture clearly teaches that life begins before birth. In the book of Psalms, David recognizes that he was a human being at the moment of conception (see Ps. 139:13–16). Other biblical texts on this topic include Genesis 25:22, Psalm 51:5, and Luke 1:41. The Bible teaches that life begins at the moment of conception. Conception is the moment when the sperm and the egg meet.

In God's eyes, a blastocyst is just as human as a seventy-year-old man. Therefore, when a couple considers birth control, it is imperative that they do not use methods that destroy life after the woman's egg has been fertilized.

3. Ibid.

We feel compelled to write to you about our findings regarding "the pill." The pill was one of the main drives of the sexual revolution back in the days of Volkswagens and large tie-dye shirts. Baby-free sex became a possibility for women, and the popularity of the pill surpassed even that of lava lamps. Society has not been the same since.

In 2010, over 100 million women were on the birth control pill.[4] Many women take the pill for purely medical reasons and are not sexually active. Certainly this is more than fine. No complaints here. But there is a powerful misconception about this "contraceptive." It is prescribed by doctors, both Christian and non-Christian, as an ethically legitimate contraception.

The pill is a very effective means of pregnancy prevention. While it is rather rare that someone becomes pregnant while on it, it is common knowledge to birth control providers that the pill is at most 99% effective—even when women consistently and accurately take it. This means that one out of every one hundred women who flawlessly use the birth control pill will get pregnant. Though this may seem like a successful method for birth control, this statistic is actually a startling and horrifying fact.

WHAT DOES THE PILL DO?

Many people, including sincere pro-life Christians, are unaware that the pill uses three types of birth-control mechanisms. The *Physicians' Desk Reference* explains the different functions of the pill.

---

4. See Nancy Gibbs, "The Pill at 50: Sex, Freedom and Paradox," *TIME*, April 22, 2010, http://content.time.com/time/magazine/article/0,9171,1983884,00.html.

Combination oral contraceptives act by suppression of gonadotropins. Although the primary mechanism of this action is inhibition of ovulation, other alterations include changes in the cervical mucus, which increase the difficulty of sperm entry into the uterus, and changes in the endometrium, which reduce the likelihood of implantation.[5]

Medical jargon aside, the pill does three things:

1. Prevents ovulation and thereby prevents conception
2. Increases mucus, which does not permit the sperm and the egg to unite
3. Thins the lining of the uterus, which can prevent a fertilized egg from implanting and thereby keep it from continuing to live

The first two mechanisms of the pill are contraceptive. If this were all that the pill accomplished, then there would be no moral controversy. However, the third mechanism of the pill is abortive in its function. The third function of the pill is to weaken the uterine wall and reduce the chances of an already fertilized egg (a human life) to implant on the wall. If the fertilized egg cannot implant, it will die.

5. Quoted in Randy Alcorn's helpful book *Does the Birth Control Pill Cause Abortions?*, rev. ed. (Sandy, OR: Eternal Perspective Ministries, 2011), 25, available online at https://www.epm.org/static/uploads/downloads/bcpill.pdf.

The following analysis of the pill's three mechanisms has been adapted from this book as well.

For a more in-depth summary of this information, you can also visit Randy Alcorn, "Does the Birth Control Pill Cause Abortions?: A Short Condensation," Eternal Perspective Ministries, February 17, 2010, http://www.epm.org/resources/2010/Feb/17/short-condensation-does-birth-control-pill-cause-a/.

HOW IS THE PILL DANGEROUS?

We would affirm the pill if it were *only* a contraceptive. A contraceptive prevents the sperm and the egg from uniting. All barrier methods such as condoms and diaphragms are true contraceptives.

An abortifacient kills the fertilized egg after it is already conceived. This is literally a life and death difference. God is explicit that murder is not morally permissible (see Ex. 20:13; Matt. 5:21–26). In light of this evidence, the question must be asked: how often do the first two mechanisms fail and the third succeed?

Every year around 420,000 babies are born in America despite their mothers taking the pill. If someone becomes pregnant while on the pill, it means that all three mechanisms of birth prevention have failed. The troubling reality is that *we do not know* how many times the first two, contraceptive mechanisms fail and the third, abortive mechanism works. We simply do not know how many times the third mechanism takes the life of an unborn child.

Randy Alcorn asks, "How many children *failed* to implant in that inhospitable environment who would have implanted in a nurturing environment unhindered by the Pill?"[6] He then postulates that if the number of deaths was twice the number of babies born, then there would be 840,000 deaths a year because of the pill.

But what if there were only 100,000 deaths a year due to the third mechanism of the pill? Or what if there were only 10 deaths a year? Would this be morally justifiable?

A husband and wife cannot play Russian roulette with a child's life every time they have sex.

6. Ibid., 102.

Lives are at stake, and we cannot sacrifice them for sexual leisure. People might think you are crazy, but please don't begin using the pill for your birth control without examining the research for yourself. If you are passionate about the sanctity of life, I am confident that you and your partner will desire to stay consistently pro-life in your marriage by avoiding the pill.

Believers must strive to glorify the Lord in every area of life. This includes even our most personal and intimate matters. Nothing is off limits to God. We have received forgiveness at the great cost of Calvary. We have been bought with a price; therefore let us glorify God in our bodies (see 1 Cor. 6:20).

Until then,
Sean and Jenny

DISCUSSION QUESTIONS

1. Do you plan on using a contraceptive in marriage? If so, what kind? It is best to decide sooner rather than later. It can take a maximum of three months for the pill to be fully gone from a woman's system once she stops taking it.
2. If there is a significant medical reason that requires you to remain on the birth-control pill, what barrier methods can you use during your week of ovulation?
3. Jenny and I strongly recommend that women visit an OB/GYN before marriage. It is good practice to have a routine medical examination before having sex. This can also be an opportunity to talk with a medical professional about any sexual difficulties you may experience that are physical in nature.

ON SEX

Sean

Dear Romantic,

I'm sure that by now you have been told a lot of different things about sex. I have met Christians who were confused by the whole experience and were really not sure what God thinks about it. I want to convince you that sex is a good creation from God and is filled with rich meaning. There are a variety of reasons why God created sexual relations, but the ultimate purpose is to magnify God. Sex is supposed to make God look incredible. It is designed to fill our hearts with worship and thanksgiving.

Understanding and applying the symbolism of sex can help you to worship. This is incredibly important for couples to understand, because it shows that sex has a purpose beyond them. In his book *Sex and the Supremacy of Christ*, John Piper writes, "God created us with sexual passion so that there would be language to describe what it means to cleave to him in love and what it means to turn away from him to others."[1] Sexual intimacy is intended by

---

1. *Sex and the Supremacy of Christ*, ed. John Piper and Justin Taylor (Wheaton, IL: Crossway, 2005), 28.

God to be symbolic of his relationship with his people. God created sex to demonstrate exclusive commitment, intimate union, and passionate pursuit and pleasure.

EXCLUSIVE COMMITMENT

Sex is intended for one man and one woman who are in a lifelong covenant relationship with each other. The Scriptures describe a husband who enters marriage as one who forsakes others and clings to his wife. "Therefore a man shall leave his father and his mother and hold fast to his wife, and they shall become one flesh" (Gen. 2:24). It is only after a man leaves his parents that he is permitted to be "one flesh" with his spouse.

These parameters of sexual activity give insight into the symbolic nature of sex. God designed sex for the confines of marriage in order to demonstrate Christ's commitment to his church. Jesus left his father in heaven in order to enter into a covenant with his bride (see John 3:16; Phil. 2:5–7).

Exclusive devotion to God is required for the Christian and was demonstrated by Christ himself. Jesus is trustworthy and will not allow just anyone to partake of his most intimate pleasures. God is exclusive in his love and will be united only to those who are exclusively devoted to him (see Luke 14:26). Sex within marriage is a picture of complete and comprehensive commitment. This picture represents the greatest commitment that Christ gives his bride.

Adultery is horrifying because it transfers sex to a context that is void of commitment and devotion. Any sexual activity outside the parameters of marriage distorts the true meaning of sex. This is why the Old Testament prophets compare sexual immorality to spiritual adultery. When we sin, we are breaking faith with God and seeking pleasure outside of our relationship with Christ.

INTIMATE UNION

Many Christians accept that marriage represents the picture of Christ and the church found in Ephesians 5:22–23. However, it is not just the covenant of marriage that reflects the gospel; it is also the sex act. When Paul writes in Ephesians 5:32 that "this mystery is profound, and I am saying that it refers to Christ and the church," he is referring to the previous verse, which mentions "the two" becoming "one flesh."

Paul is saying that the mystery of the gospel is displayed within both the marriage covenant and the marriage bed. In 1 Corinthians 6:16–17 he continues this teaching when he writes, "For, as it is written, 'The two will become one flesh.' But he who is joined to the Lord becomes one spirit with him." Paul is comparing the sexual union of a man and woman with the union between a Christian and God.

When a believer is joined to the Lord, he becomes one with Christ. The word *joined* is literally translated "holds fast," which is the same language used in Genesis 2:24 and Deuteronomy 10:20. The sexual union between a husband and wife represents the union between Christ and his church.

For a couple to become naked in front of each other requires a level of relationship that is free of shame and guilt. The sexual act within marriage symbolically shows the intimacy that a believer has with Christ, which is both gentle and tender and yet bold and free. When a husband and wife accept each other's naked bodies, they are accepting each other despite imperfections. "And the man and his wife were both naked and were not ashamed" (Gen. 2:25). Every human being has physical and relational imperfections, but there is no need for us to fear or be ashamed. Spouses should welcome each other fully in the same way that Christ invites his church to enjoy intimacy with him.

Christ's invitation for us to enjoy him is full of grace and joy that covers all blemishes (see Heb. 4:14–16).

PASSIONATE PURSUIT AND PLEASURE

God is willing to sacrifice his own Son in order to remove any hindrance between him and the church. The passion of romance and the sexual experience depicts the love of Christ for his elect. This story of romance is told in the Song of Songs, where the king is able to conquer every objection that the woman has about intimacy (see Song 1:6, 8–10; 2:9–15; 3:1–3; 5:2–3). Jim Hamilton is correct in saying that "the Song of Songs sings of the Davidic king who overcomes the alienation and distance between himself and his ideal bride to enjoy one flesh intimacy in a lush garden and in Zion."[2] Sex may not be easy at first, but each partner should selflessly and patiently seek to overcome any obstacles, whether physical or emotional.

Sex within marriage can be both passionate and pleasurable. The physical pleasure of sex points to the delight that Christians experience in being united to Christ. Sex also tells the story of the character of God. The church is able to take delight in God while God also takes pleasure in them. "The LORD your God is in your midst, a mighty one who will save; he will rejoice over you with gladness; he will quiet you by his love; he will exult over you with loud singing" (Zeph. 3:17). Jesus is on a mission to win over his bride and has gone to great lengths in order to accomplish this. Christ initiates romance with his bride and overcomes all hindrances to bring her into his chamber.

---

2. James M. Hamilton Jr., *God's Glory in Salvation through Judgment: A Biblical Theology* (Wheaton, IL: Crossway, 2010), 305.

HOW IS IT NURTURED?

The symbolic significance of sex has practical implications for how a healthy sexual relationship is nurtured in marriage. One of the ways for you to begin honoring God in sex is by cultivating a thankful heart for your spouse. An exclusive commitment is strengthened by a genuine delight in your spouse. Ephesians 5:4–5 compares and contrasts sexual immorality with thanksgiving. Thanking God for your spouse and remembering his or her areas of growth is one way to nurture your relationship. Contentment is key when you are cultivating joy and delight. Scripture calls us to take delight in the spouse God has given us and to enjoy him or her exclusively. This includes being physically attracted to your spouse (see Prov. 5:19).

This means that sex is more than a feeling. It is about obedience to Christ. Sex should not be viewed as drudgery but should be modeled as delightful. It should never be withheld for selfish gain but should be offered freely, with grace and generosity. In these ways, sex is a picture of the mystery of the gospel. By seeking to glorify God in our bodies (see 1 Cor. 6:20), we experience joy, bless our spouses, and magnify Christ.

EVANGELISTIC INVITATION

If it is true that sex is laced with gospel symbolism, then it is also true that sex has an evangelistic appeal. A vibrant sexual life is a sign of a healthy marriage. Sex is evangelistic in the sense that such intimacy impacts a marriage relationship in a noticeable way. The outside world should be able to tell that you have been with your spouse (by your loyalty, joy, contentment, and so on) just as they should be able to tell when someone has been with Jesus.

Another common way that sex symbolizes the gospel is through the offspring produced through a couple's union. Just as a wife bears fruit when she is united to her husband, we bear fruit of the Spirit when we are united with Christ. Even if someone is infertile physically, this painful experience has the potential to be winsome to the world by demonstrating hope in a perfect world to come. The new heavens and new earth will not be broken. Sex is simply a shadow of the reality to come.

Never forget that the most enjoyable act of sex cannot compare to the endless joys of fellowship with God in heaven (see Ps. 16:11).

Until then,
Sean

DISCUSSION QUESTIONS

1. What are four reasons that God created sex?
2. Are you nervous about having sex with your spouse? Why or why not?
3. What are your expectations about sex?
4. Have you talked with a mentor and your future spouse about your sexual history? If not, be sure to read chapters 10, 15, and 16 in Sean Perron and Spencer Harmon, *Letters to a Romantic: On Dating* (Phillipsburg, NJ: P&R, 2017).
5. For further reading, see C. J. Mahaney, *Sex, Romance, and the Glory of God: What Every Christian Husband Needs to Know* (Wheaton, IL: Crossway, 2004).

PREPARING FOR YOUR
WEDDING NIGHT

Sean

Dear Romantic,

My goal in this letter is to help you plan specifically for your wedding night. Please don't read it until the week before your wedding. Although you may be curious about the contents of this letter, there is no need for you to read it before then. (However, if you have a sexual history that you haven't shared with anyone yet, it is imperative that you do so before your wedding.[1] Previous sexual sin, especially pornography, can initially hinder sex. This does not have to be the case. Christ accomplished full redemption that can be applied specifically to you and to any situation you are in.)

As you know, first comes love, then comes marriage, then

---

1. For more information about how and when to talk about sexual history, read chapters 10, 15, and 16 in Sean Perron and Spencer Harmon, *Letters to a Romantic: On Dating* (Phillipsburg, NJ: 2017).

comes sex. It is unfortunate that most churches neglect this topic and do the body of Christ harm. It is equally frustrating when other churches use explicitly crude language and talk about sex in unhelpful ways. In contrast to both of these approaches, Jesus wants Christians to think biblically about sex.

Many things could be said in this letter, but I want to focus on the *attitude* that should shape our view of sexual activity. The gospel has no boundaries and is not privy to categories like "public" or "private." Jesus is the God of the living room and of the bedroom. This is good news. God has everyone's best interests at heart. Selfishness in any area, including our most intimate endeavors, is detrimental to our joy.

On your wedding night and on every night after, your mind should be that of Christ Jesus, who, although being in the form of God, did not consider equality with God something to be grasped, but made himself nothing, taking on the very nature of a servant (see Phil. 2:5–7). Before you lie down in bed with your spouse, you must be willing to lay your life down for him or her. We need the grace of Jesus in order to do this.

Your sex drive should be selfless. God wants to maximize your pleasure by rooting it both in God and in bringing your spouse pleasure. When you think of your wedding night, what are your thoughts centered on? Are you primarily concerned about your sexual gratification or your spouse's? Are you worried about experiencing the perfect orgasm, or are you excited to help your spouse climax? Which comes first in your mind?

I encourage you to determine in your heart to serve your spouse sexually instead of yourself. Make it your goal to have him or her satisfied before you are. Make it your plan to help them feel comfortable, loved, cared for, and honored on the first night of marriage. You should get a kick out of coming up with ways to love them. Your goal should be to outdo the other in kindness.

Many couples are nervous on their wedding night and are not sure what to expect when it comes to sex. This is common and is nothing to be ashamed of. In fact, this is something to be cherished and is wonderfully beautiful. In order to serve your spouse selflessly, I suggest crafting a plan for the evening.

BEFORE SEX

First, how can you make your spouse feel as comfortable as possible before sex? Depending on the time of your ceremony, should you have a nice dinner after the wedding reception? Should you go for a private walk after the reception and remind them of the top ten reasons you are ecstatic to be married to them? When you arrive at your hotel room for the night, how can you put them at ease? Is there special music you can play to set a gentle tone and calm them? Would your spouse enjoy a massage with lotion that contains his or her favorite fragrance? Or would your spouse enjoy spending some time in prayer before you tenderly kiss each other?

If you are nervous about your wedding night, set your mind on various ways you can serve your spouse in order to calm *your soul*. Direct all your attention to caring for him or her. Sit beside the soothing streams of selfless service and let them wash over you. Don't occupy your mind with every possible outcome or previous failure. Captivate your heart with a Christ-filled joy, and love with abandonment. Let Psalm 131 turn your confidence and hope to the Lord.

> O LORD, my heart is not lifted up;
>   my eyes are not raised too high;
> *I do not occupy myself with things*
>   *too great and too marvelous for me.*

But I have *calmed* and *quieted* my soul,
   like a weaned child with its mother;
   like a weaned child is my soul within me.
O Israel, *hope in the* LORD
   from this time forth and forevermore.

DURING SEX

Second, how can you serve your spouse during sex? The best advice that our marriage counselors gave us for our wedding night was to communicate verbally before, during, and after sex. Talk to each other the entire time. Ask questions in order to see how your spouse is doing. Ask them, "Is this okay if I do this?" "Can I place my hand here?" "How are you doing?" "Are you comfortable?" "How does this feel?"

Make statements that express your deep love for your spouse. Tell them how beautiful or handsome they are. Let them know what feels good. Whisper sweet words that you have always wanted to share with them. A helpful exercise might be to read through the Song of Songs the week before your wedding and to come up with some poetical ways you can express your pleasure in them.

The goal with these questions and expressions is to begin thinking of ways that you can serve and honor your spouse. The goal of your wedding night is not to have a fury of passion that culminates quickly, like a techno dance party. The goal is to serve with the fruit of the Spirit—love, joy, peace, patience, kindness, goodness, faithfulness, gentleness, and self-control.

AFTER SEX

Finally, how can you serve your partner after sex? It is possible that your partner may not climax sexually on your wedding night. You should not be crushed or caught off guard by this. Instead, you should make it your goal to find ways to please your spouse, set your mind on them with delight, and help them to have an orgasm during the honeymoon.

Each time you come together sexually the following week, take delight in exhibiting *patience, gentleness,* and *self-control.* When you are manifesting these fruits, there is no law or condemnation (see Gal. 5:22–23). View each sexual encounter as a learning experience and a gift to enjoy. Remember, there is no rush. Spend time getting to know your spouse and all the ways that they find pleasure. Time is on your side, and sex will only get sweeter.

Because the Christian should not act out of selfish ambition or vain conceit, the marriage bed must remain undefiled by lust. This automatically rules out performing any sexual act that would bring harm to your partner. If you desire a sexual experience that inappropriately harms the body, you must immediately put that desire to death. Honoring your spouse also means not asking them to perform sexual acts they do not enjoy. For example, if your spouse finds French kissing disgusting, then it should be your instinct to avoid it—not because it is wrong to place a tongue in a mouth, but because it isn't your spouse's preference. The goal is to honor them and perform sexual acts that they enjoy.

Questions frequently arise when one partner wants to have oral sex. Scripture does not forbid oral sex—but this is not the issue. If both of you enjoy oral sex and can thank God for it, then have as much as you want as long as you don't find yourselves neglecting intercourse. However, if your spouse feels uncomfortable with it because of his or her past, or simply because of preference, then Jesus Christ wants you to outdo your partner in kindness by putting your desires away. The God of heaven wants you to have all the pleasure you can find as long as you are being selfless. This is why only Christians can have truly satisfying sex. Only the Christian couple can find their delight in selfless service. It is only the Christian husband or wife who can satisfy both their body and heart in the marriage bed.

Though it may sound strange now, remember to have sex often. You and your spouse will need to work together to make sure that sex is a priority in your schedule. Most people don't realize that the Bible actually commands married couples to come together sexually on a regular basis. Paul writes,

> But because of the temptation to sexual immorality, each man should have his own wife and each woman her own husband. The husband should give to his wife her conjugal rights, and likewise the wife to her husband. For the wife does not have authority over her own body, but the husband does. Likewise the husband does not have authority over his own body, but the wife does. *Do not deprive one another, except perhaps by agreement for a limited time, that you may devote yourselves to prayer; but then come together again, so that Satan may not tempt you because of your lack of self-control.* (1 Cor. 7:2–5)

It is amazing that Satan wants to keep you from sex. The irony is thick—the Devil wants you to have sex before marriage, but he wants to keep you from having sex in marriage. God wants just the opposite: for you to preserve your purity before your wedding but to have frequent sex once you are married.

During your honeymoon, go ahead and make a plan to have sex on a regular basis with your spouse once you return to your normal routines. Make sure it is frequent. As a couple, decide whether this will be two, three, or four or more times a week.

As you plan, be sure to keep the Devil at bay by surprising your spouse with sex and by flirting like you have never flirted before.

Settle in your heart now to make your marital bliss completely selfless. Above all, remember to love your neighbor as yourself—especially the one who will sleep next to you.

Until then,
Sean

DISCUSSION QUESTIONS

1. What emotions come to mind when you think about your wedding night?
2. Write down specific ways you can serve your partner before sex.
3. Write down specific ways you can serve your partner during sex.
4. Write down specific ways you can serve your partner after sex.
5. Will you be crushed emotionally if sex is more difficult than you expected?
6. Who is a trustworthy and godly couple you can talk to about these things before your wedding? Who can you call on the phone during your honeymoon if you and your spouse are having difficulty with sex?

MORE THAN SEX

Sean

Dear Future Husband,

If I wanted to embrace a stereotype, I would say that your fiancée struggles with insecurity about her physical beauty while you struggle with dwelling too much on that beauty. Or, to say it another way, she doesn't think that her outward appearance is enough, but you have thought about it more than enough.

The temptation for everyone to dwell on outward appearance is real. Man dwells on the outward appearance, but God looks at the heart (see 1 Sam. 16:7). We all have a natural tendency to walk by sight instead of by faith (see 2 Cor. 5:7). It is all too common for us to focus on what is visible instead of what is invisible.

Listen to how the Bible describes beautiful women.

> Do not let your adorning be external—the braiding of hair and the putting on of gold jewelry, or the clothing you wear— but let your adorning be the hidden person of the heart with the imperishable beauty of a gentle and quiet spirit, which in

God's sight is very precious. For this is how the holy women who hoped in God used to adorn themselves, by submitting to their own husbands, as Sarah obeyed Abraham, calling him lord. And you are her children, if you do good and do not fear anything that is frightening. (1 Peter 3:3–6)

The Bible's emphasis is not on the external. Its emphasis is on the adornment of the heart, which is very precious in God's sight. What is pretty in your sight? What do you find very precious? How will you help your bride to realize that she has value? How will you balance out your thoughts in a biblical way?

REMIND HER

First, remind her that she is beautiful because she is made in the image of God. Before you brush over this, let this reality sink in. God does not make trash. He crafts pieces of art that are worthy of the finest museums. "So God created man in his own image, in the image of God he created him; male and female he created them" (Gen. 1:27). The image of God is not just a nice notion to make unattractive people feel better about themselves. God says he created men and women in his image, and we should not let this reality become just a trite saying. Christ has made a personal claim on his creation. If you scoff at his art, you insult him.

There is a real, holy, stunning way in which your fiancée is unwaveringly beautiful because she reflects God. God himself is the definition of beauty, and therefore anything that has his fingerprint is gorgeous. The fall in Genesis 3 did not remove the image of God from humanity (see James 3:9). Even if your wife is marred by third-degree burns or ransacked by leprosy, this reality is unshaken: every day her image pours forth the speech of God's handiwork.

REMIND YOURSELF

Second, remind yourself of the hidden image of God made possible in Christ. It is good to tell your fiancée that she is pretty, but do not miss out on the thrill of praising her hidden person. Physical appearance is fleeting, but there is an imperishable beauty that only gets better. If she is growing in faith, courage, gentleness, holy submission, and compassion, make it a point to praise these ornaments. The fruit of the Spirit has a sweetness that will never sour. Dwell on her godly character, and attach your heart to it!

Ask the Lord to give you eyes to behold true beauty. Beg him to give you grace to truly appreciate the grace he has given her. Make it your top priority to value, treasure, and be drawn to her godly character. Look hard for and love her invisible pearls. They are formed perfectly by the oyster of the gospel. Her inner heart is a gorgeous glimpse of God.

Outward beauty is wonderfully fleeting. As she gets older, her every wrinkle will help accent the eternal radiance found in her heart. Do not miss out on enjoying the realities that will never perish. Remind her that she is made in the image of God, and encourage her to continue looking more like Christ in godly character. And let me tell you a secret: the more you cultivate an attraction for her godly character, the more fruit she will produce. The more you water a flower, the brighter it will bloom.

Until then,
Sean

DISCUSSION QUESTIONS

1. How much time do you spend thinking about your fiancée? How much of that time is spent thinking about her physical appearance compared to your time spent thinking about her spiritual beauty?
2. List ten reasons why your future spouse will be beautiful when she is seventy-five years old.

WAITING FOR YOUR WEDDING

Sean

Dear Romantic,

You are one day closer to marriage and one day closer to the return of Jesus. There is a link between these two things: just as you long to be with your future spouse in an unhindered and unrestrained way, you should long to be with your Savior as well, free from sin and unrestrained by the flesh.

Just as you have waited all these years for your wedding day and your life together, I pray that you eagerly await to behold the face of Jesus and spend eternity with him. Your spouse is going to walk down the aisle to meet you because you have longed for each other. Jesus is going to descend from the sky to meet those who have loved him and awaited his return. The apostle Paul writes about this anticipation,

> Henceforth there is laid up for me the crown of righteous-
> ness, which the Lord, the righteous judge, will award to me

on that day, and not only to me but also to all who have loved his appearing. (2 Tim. 4:8)

Waiting for our blessed hope, the appearing of the glory of our great God and Savior Jesus Christ . . . (Titus 2:13)

At the beginning of my engagement to Jenny, people would ask me, "What day are you thinking about getting married?" I would respond, "Tomorrow" or "Yesterday." I assume you are like me and can hardly wait. Toward the end of our engagement, people would ask, "Are you excited?" This question became wonderfully foolish because the answer was so obvious. I assume the same is true for you.

I do not say this to be overly spiritual, but the only thing more exciting than your upcoming wedding day is the return of Jesus. We can say this only because Jesus has been kind to our hearts and because we have tasted and seen that the Lord is good (see Ps. 34:8). His steadfast love is better than marriage (see Ps. 63:3).

Now you might be tempted to think, *If Jesus comes back before I am married, will I have missed out?* The thought of missing out on the joy, friendship, or intimacy of marriage might leave you feeling depressed. Take heart. As John Piper beautifully writes, "Nothing is lost. The music of every pleasure is transposed into an infinitely higher key."[1]

Or, to think of it visually, we would never trade a person for a photo. Marriage is simply a picture of the person and work of Jesus Christ; marriage is only a mirror that reflects the relationship of Jesus and his bride; marriage is merely a good gift to

---

1. John Piper, *This Momentary Marriage: A Parable of Permanence* (Wheaton, IL: Crossway, 2012), 15.

glorify a satisfying God. Enjoy marriage, but only as it submits to the supreme pleasure of knowing God. For, while now we see in a mirror dimly, soon we shall see face-to-face (see 1 Cor. 13:12).

Until then,
Sean

DISCUSSION QUESTIONS

1. How often do you think about the return of Jesus?
2. Does your wedding day give you more joy than the return of Christ? Why or why not?

CONCLUSION

FINAL LETTERS

Sean and Spencer

Dear Romantic,

As Sean and I were putting the final touches on the manuscript of this book, my father suddenly and shockingly died. No one expected it, and my family and I are still picking up the shattered pieces of our hearts and trying to put our lives back together. Our hearts feel sick under the weight of our grief. My dad was excited about this book and wanted to read it—and I wanted him to read it, too.

It struck me during the days surrounding my dad's death how deeply connected Taylor was to this tragedy. She prayed with a trembling and tearful voice in the car while holding my hand. Her gentle touch on my elbow comforted me as I greeted family, friends, and strangers at the funeral. She held me through deep and groaning sobs late at night as the waves of the reality of my father's death rolled over me. My grief was her grief.

When I first married Taylor, I wasn't thinking about my father's death. However, it struck me during this time that, when

I married Taylor, I was choosing the person who would stand with me at my father's funeral. I was covenanting with the person who would weep with me, rejoice with me, laugh with me, and challenge me. I wasn't thinking about the dark nights of my soul when I got on one knee and asked Taylor to be my wife.

Yet the times of my deepest gratitude for my wife have been the times of my deepest trial. There's so much more to marriage than the wedding day, so much more to romance than dates and flowers. My wife is my fellow pilgrim in the valley of the shadow of death. She bears with me the pangs and blows of the jagged curse on this world. Taylor has had an inestimable impact on the way I view my life, my trials, my ministry, and my mission. This is because these aspects are no longer *mine*; they are *ours*.

So, as you endeavor toward the altar, be glad and rejoice in your spouse. Yet also remember that you are covenanting with the one who will walk by you for better or *for worse*. The person whom you marry is the one who will be with you in the deepest sorrows and trials of your life. You want a spouse who will help keep your eyes on Christ when you walk through fiery trials. Who do you want with you at a funeral?

Our feeble attempt in this book has been to equip you to think biblically about engagement, because life is too short and Jesus is too wonderful not to listen to the guiding voice of our Good Shepherd. This season right before marriage is so crucial for you and your fiancé because you are preparing for a lifetime of faithfulness to each other—for better or for worse. The deepest joys and deepest sorrows await you on the other side of the altar, and you are not alone.

As I stood in front of my father's casket, dazed that our lives had taken such an unexpected turn, I felt the gentle touch of my wife's hand in mine. Her presence was only an echo of the deeper presence of Christ with me in this trial. And as my wife and I continue to walk through these trials together, recalling God's promises in the darkest valleys, we reverberate with the rhythms of the gospel. We display the ancient story of Christ and the church. This is the great story in which each marriage finds its meaning. My prayer is that in this story you and your future spouse will find solid ground for your relationship as you traverse the mountains of joy and the valleys of sorrow.

Until then,
Spencer

Dear Romantic,

There is a great multitude of men and women who have gone before us: godly relationships, beautiful marriages, and stories dripping with the sweet fragrance of God. Yet every sweeping romance story must come to an end. Death is inevitable. Some stories carry on throughout the years and pass away peacefully on a bedside. Others are jarred unexpectedly and brought to a screeching halt by sudden tragedy.

To be honest, I feel totally inadequate to write to you on such a topic as the death of a loved one. I cannot imagine losing the wife of my youth. The thought of Jenny dying is something I cannot yet fathom and something for which I barely know how to prepare.

While I was pursuing Jenny, a dear friend would often remind me about the brevity of life. He would say things like, "Hold the things of this world loosely, Sean. Do not cling to them too tightly. Don't make Jennifer an idol. Christ is sufficient, and soon everything else shall pass away." His words have stuck with me, and they resurface in my mind from time to time.

This world is fading, and along with it even the most precious gifts. There will come a time when the brown eyes of my bride will grow dim and her soft hands will go limp. Thoughts of this future moisten my eyes and press against my heart. And, if I am not careful, my world could become as dark as the inside of her casket.

The only thing that brings me hope in the midst of such thoughts is the gospel of Jesus. This world is not my home. Nor is it the home of my bride. Marriage is a wonderful thing, but it is not the most beautiful thing. There is something sweeter than her lips and more precious than her smile.

You too will soon lock your arms with a fellow pilgrim. You will soon whisper love into the ear of a sojourner (see 1 Peter 2:11). Live this life holding the hand of your spouse loosely, ready and willing to offer his or her hand back to Jesus. Do not fight death, for Christ has already conquered it.

Jesus has prepared a place for your spouse to dwell. If it were not so, he would have told you (see John 14:2). Honor him, and "let those who have wives live as though they had none" (1 Cor. 7:29). Love your wife by "hating" her (see Luke 14:26). These are such odd sayings of Jesus and Paul, aren't they? Yet they stick in the mind and guard the soul from clinging too closely to this world.

It is a joy and an unexpected gift from God to be engaged. It is a joy and a cherished delight to walk through life hand in hand with your best friend. Do not fear death or let it rob you of the happiness of glorifying God today.

Glorify God by enjoying him *in* all things and *above* all things. Both are possible, and the Bible commands such happiness in our lives. Glorify God by enjoying the moments he has given you and the gifts he has bestowed upon you.

"Enjoy life with the wife whom you love, all the days of

your vain life that he has given you under the sun, because that is your portion in life and in your toil at which you toil under the sun" (Eccl. 9:9). Laugh with your future spouse, flirt to the appropriate fullness, and buy chocolates and flowers. But be satisfied in God above all these things. Dig your joy deep into what cannot be taken away. Dip your bucket into the eternal pleasures of God, and drink from his fountain, which never dries.

There will come a day for each of us when life will stand still and a grave will be occupied. We will mourn like we have never mourned before. But we will not despair like the world does (see 1 Thess. 4:13). We have a loving Father who grants eternal hope and raises the dead.

On that day, we will be grateful that he gave us the grace to enjoy precious moments on earth and to ground our hope in him above all. So for now, enjoy him *in* all things and *above* all things. Or, to say it a different way for marriage, squeeze her hand tightly, but hold it loosely.

Until then,
Sean

ACKNOWLEDGMENTS

This book would not have been possible without the assistance of others. Numerous pastors, friends, and family members have contributed to this project in ways that they don't even realize. Many of our thoughts and ideas have come from other people, and we are especially indebted to godly mentors in our lives. The influence of Heath Lambert and John Piper on this book is obvious and cannot be overstated.

The Association of Certified Biblical Counselors and P&R have graciously supported this book, and we are deeply humbled by their enthusiasm for the project. We especially want to thank those who read the manuscript in advance and provided valuable feedback. Some of those people include Ben and Naomi Fennell, Nate and Jana Grote, Brad Taunton, Brennan Kolbe, Renee Hoskins, Ruth Anne Irvin, Amanda Martin, Samuel James, Kaity Glick, Rebecca Maketansky, and Amy Evenson.

Sean especially wants to thank his parents, Steve and Annie, as well as his in-laws, Greg and Laura Whiteaker, for their prayers and constant encouragement. Spencer would like to thank his mom, Patty Harmon, and to honor his father, John Harmon, who passed away before the publication of this book.

His in-laws, Steve and Ruth Thompson, also gave their feedback for several chapters of the book.

Above all else, we want to thank our wives, who gave sacrificially in order to make this endeavor possible. They gave priceless time and energy in order to bring this project to fruition. Their love, wisdom, and sacrifice are irreplaceable and have not gone unnoticed. They truly model the gospel of Jesus Christ.

It is our prayer that this book will advance the Great Commission of Jesus Christ, who is the Lord and Savior of the world. He deserves all praise, and we cannot praise him enough.

Sean Perron graduated with his MDiv from The Southern Baptist Theological Seminary and is currently chief of staff at the Association of Certified Biblical Counselors (ACBC). He and his wife Jennifer live in Jacksonville, Florida.

Spencer Harmon is pastor at Vine Street Baptist Church in Louisville, Kentucky. He and his wife Taylor have two daughters.

Together Sean and Spencer write on their website: www.unspokenblog.org.

Association of Certified
Biblical Counselors

Since 1976, the Association of Certified Biblical Counselors (ACBC) has been training and certifying biblical counselors to ensure excellence in the counseling room by faithfulness to the Word of God. We offer a comprehensive biblical counseling certification program that is rigorous, but attainable by even the busiest pastor or church member. Our certification process is made up of three phases: learning, exams and application, and supervision.

ACBC has grown from a handful of individuals to thousands of certified counselors all around the world. Now in our fourth decade of pursuing excellence in biblical counseling, we have had five executive directors: Dr. Bob Smith, Dr. Howard Eyrich, Rev. Bill Goode, and Rev. Randy Patten. Dr. Heath Lambert became the fifth executive director in 2013.

Every Christian is called to speak the truth in love to one another. ACBC trains Christians in their gospel responsibility to be disciple-makers and to build up the body of Christ. This training is accomplished through conferences and events throughout the world.

For more information about ACBC and biblical counseling resources, visit www.biblicalcounseling.com.